RETIRING
ON
YOUR OWN
· TERMS ·

RETIRING ON YOUR OWN ·TERMS·

Your Total Retirement Planning Guide to Finances, Health, Life-style, and Much, Much More

By James W. Ellison; Doris Reardon;
Michael L. Freedman, M.D.;
Herbert Mayo, Ph.D.; and
Robert F. Palmerton

CROWN PUBLISHERS, INC. ▪ NEW YORK

ACKNOWLEDGMENTS

The authors would like to express their appreciation for the materials and expertise of Oscar M. Kreigman, Ph.D. The authors would also like to thank their editors, James O'Shea Wade and Jane von Mehren, whose concerned interest combined with broad experience has been most helpful. James Ellison is particularly grateful to the Writers Room, which provided him with both space and valued friendships during the writing of this book.

Excerpts from *Investments: An Introduction* by Herbert Mayo. All rights reserved. Used by permission of The Dryden Press, a division of Holt, Rinehart & Winston, Inc.

Published by Crown Publishers, Inc., 201 East 50th Street, New York, New York 10022

CROWN is a trademark of Crown Publishers, Inc.
Manufactured in the United States of America

Library of Congress Cataloging-in-Publication Data

Retiring on your own terms.

  Includes index.
  1. Retirement—Planning.   2.   Retirement income—
Planning.   I. Ellison, James Whitfield.
HQ1062.P626   1989   646.7′9   88-20343
ISBN 0-517-57130-7
10 9 8 7 6 5 4 3

Contents

C O N T E N T S

RETIRING
ON
YOUR OWN
·TERMS·

Introduction

It is not generally realized that retirement as an institution is fairly new—new enough that the Conference Board speaks of "the retirement revolution." New enough that only a generation ago the nation's wage and salary earners tended to stay on their jobs until the advent of disablement or death. Even when the Social Security Act of 1935 first established a public system of supplemental financial assistance at age 65, the impact was by no means as great, numerically, as one might suppose, for the average person at that time only lived to be 62½ years old.

Today, thanks in large part to our extraordinary advances in longevity and health, the United States is becoming a four-generation society for the first time in its history. By the year 2000, one in every seven or eight people will be 65 or older if longevity continues to increase at the present pace.

"As more and more Americans reach age 65 in better shape than any previous generation," wrote Sylvia Porter in a newspaper series on the subject, "the stereotypes of old age, still believed by so many uninformed among us, are simply disappearing." Instead, the reality now gaining wide recognition among experts in the field is that age—like youth—has a number of different phases. The first of these, often called "senior adulthood," is defined as the period from 65 to perhaps 80 during which increasing numbers of retirees are vigorous and independent and can fill important roles in community and national life. A University of Chicago gerontologist sees this group as "an enormous resource that has just begun to be tapped."

The advertising/marketing/communications community has been quick to join the chorus. "What's new? Old people!" trumpets the trade journal *Sales and Marketing Management*. And *Newsweek* takes note of the new media approach: "Gone is the dogma that middle-aged people are sexless, hopeless and resistant to change."

There are new or newly updated magazines, with rising circulations: *Prime Time, 50 Plus, Modern Maturity, Dynamic Years, New England Senior Citizen, Retirement Life,* and the like. In fact, publications directed toward those approaching retirement age, known in this book as *Pre-REtirement Planners*, are now numerous enough to be listed under a separate category in magazine directories. Weekly television dramas now include more mature people in leading roles. These efforts to reach and tap the Maturity Market serve to make a point of great meaning in terms of retirement today. For as older Americans find themselves "fashionable"—that is to say, courted and wooed, paid attention to, generally depicted in attractive and functional roles—it follows that they will also be moving out of the backwaters of national life into the broad mainstream. It also follows that retirement will become vastly more important than at any time in the past, not only to the retiree but to society at large, and that the planning for it will be as crucial for those in their 50s and 60s—and even in their late 40s—as a college education is for our youth.

In 1981, in the midst of growing "gray power," CBS created and launched the Pre-Retirement Education Program (PREP), a unique contribution to a relatively unexplored area of concern for increasing numbers of people. Over the past seven years PREP has been attended by several thousand CBS employees and their spouses. In fact, spouses are urged to participate in the seminars in order to have a common basis for decisions in such crucial matters as financial planning, company benefits, health, where to live after retirement, use of leisure time, and second careers. With each passing year, PREP has reinforced its reputation as *the* model for successful pre-retirement planning.

We are now pleased to be able to offer the heart of the CBS

seminar, in vastly extended book form, to *Pre-REtirement Planners* everywhere. In the pages and sections that follow, we will help think you through your retirement stage by stage while you acquire data, examine options, and sort out your plans for this next—and vital—phase of your life.

First and foremost in every *Pre-REtirement Planner's* mind is the question of money. The new economics of retirement have to be learned, and as you learn them you will be reaching toward your all-important objective: *how to maintain your pre-retirement standard of living for the rest of your life.*

Consider this book a rehearsal for retirement. "Ideally," according to the program director of the Institute of Gerontology at the University of Michigan, "people ought to practice living on their retirement income, and replacing work with other meaningful activity, ahead of time." In other words, open the show out of town. It makes sense because—to extend the metaphor just a bit further—each person writes the script for his or her own retirement. By testing it out, you learn valuable lessons about how well it's going to play.

So, as retirement rehearsal . . .

1. Practice living on your estimated retirement income, after business expenses.

2. Start developing some of the retirement activities you think will interest you. There are contacts to make and research to do, whether you have in mind volunteer work, further education, or a second career.

3. If you plan to move, learn everything you can about your prospective new home. It's not likely that you will be able to move repeatedly, nor would you want to, so spend time, if you can, in the new community, during the off-season if there is one. Talk to people who live there; keep looking for disadvantages. You already know the advantages, because they're what attracted you in the first place.

4. Strengthen relationships *outside* the business environment—with family, friends, and neighbors.

5. Check how long it takes you to do various activities around the house or yard that you look forward to doing in retirement. You may think there are enough chores to keep you busy forever, but you'll

probably zip right through them in a few weeks and then have to start looking for something else to keep you occupied.

6. As important as working out a viable financial future is the planning you and your spouse can do in anticipation of your retirement. Couples who have lived together in the evenings, on weekends, and during vacations for virtually all their married lives don't necessarily find it easy, especially at first, to be together all day, every day. You and your spouse might want to talk together about seemingly minor potential irritants.

Here are a few tips for you married *Pre-REtirement Planners*:

• Plan finances together. Money planning will cushion stress.

• Plan separate activities. Assure privacy for each other.

• Respect each other's routines, friends, and conversations.

• Develop some common interests, from hobbies to sports to work on a political or community campaign. Such activities help stimulate each other's involvement and assure you of continuing things to talk about and plan for.

• Keep your lines of communication open. In retirement, you will be talking with each other more than ever before.

We will be exploring the above subjects in detail in this handbook. Here you will find specifics, not generalities; case studies to serve as examples, not just overviews. The principal objective is to improve the *quality* of your retirement by helping you to make decisions now. These are decisions that you will review at least on a yearly basis until you retire, continually making adjustments for changing conditions. Even if your retirement is only a few years, or months, ahead, *Retiring on Your Own Terms* should be an invaluable aid in helping you to plan the most satisfying retirement possible!

RETIRING
ON
YOUR OWN
·TERMS·

Part 1

PLANNING FOR YOUR FINANCIAL
INDEPENDENCE

1

Setting Your Objectives
for Financial Independence

Planning for your financial independence is not difficult once you learn the secret of how to do it. Most of us plan for our financial future in a number of informal ways. We watch the balances of our savings accounts as we make deposits and add interest; we force ourselves to save through various payroll deduction plans; we look for safety together with the highest yields (interest rates and dividends) in stocks, bonds, and mutual funds; and at the heart of our investments is the hope that they will increase our wealth over a period of perhaps several years.

What most of our plans lack, however, is organization, and one of the chief purposes of this book is to help you establish an overall objective for a financially healthy retirement and then provide you with a system for achieving that objective. Remember that one critical proposition underlies all of the issues, problems, and opportunities of retirement, which can be stated as follows: *The quality of your retirement depends on your ability to maintain your pre-retirement standard of living for the rest of your life.*

In other words, you must plan your future in such a way that you can achieve financial independence.

But is it reasonable to expect that you can maintain your pre-retirement standard of living once you no longer have a job, business, or professional practice and you're reduced to living on a retirement income? The answer can be a resounding yes! Maintaining your pre-retirement standard of living for the rest of your life doesn't mean that you will need exactly the same amount of before-tax (federal, state, and local) income; it means that you will achieve exactly the same purchasing power that you had immediately before retirement.

Your particular—and unique—retirement income objective will be expressed in the form of a specific amount of annual income after retirement. We will work closely together to determine what that amount should be; it is an amount that will be influenced by a number of variables. These include your present and projected family income, your present age and the age at which you plan to retire, an estimate of when your spouse will retire, and your dependents and their ages. We'll explore these variables in more detail later.

Ideally, you will retire voluntarily at precisely the time you wish—you may decide to take early retirement at 62 or retirement with full Social Security benefits at 65, or even later or earlier retirement depending on needs, goals, and family pressures and problems. Unhappily, however, some of us will be forced to retire at a time we have not chosen or adequately prepared for. Our companies are sold, merged, liquidated, or restructured in such a way that many older employees are suddenly faced with the reality of early retirement neither planned for nor expected. All the more reason to plan early and carefully for your financial independence. Nothing is certain in this life except death and taxes—certainly not your job security!

To help you toward your goal of financial independence, we are going to work with you to develop a financial plan. In the following pages, you will receive the information you need to achieve your financial independence at your normal retirement age, which we assume is 65, and at an earlier retirement age, 62. You will also have enough information to figure out what alternative actions may be necessary if your retirement plans are suddenly changed.

The variables can be considerable, and for this effort to have real meaning it is necessary to make certain assumptions—principal among them that there will be an annual inflation rate of 5 percent. A sage has suggested that if we were to ask three leading economists what the rate of inflation will average over the next ten years, we would receive three different answers. Five percent is reasonable as an average because it is a little higher than the annual inflation rate experienced since World War

II. You must understand, however, that you have made an assumption, nothing more; if conditions change, your retirement income will have to be replanned to fit the new reality.

Another important ground rule to follow is not to immerse yourself too deeply in the detail of your estimates. You can spend hours adding up columns, including pennies, and come up with a ridiculously specific figure such as $927.63, or, more appropriately, you can round everything to the nearest hundred or thousand and spend minutes adding the same data. You might possibly have a difference of a few hundred dollars by rounding off your figures, but when you recognize all the assumptions that have to be made, any kind of tight precision is impossible. Our objective is to determine how close we can get to the retirement income objective—that is, your estimated retirement expenses. Once we have done that we will determine what actions can be taken to cover any gaps between retirement expenses and income.

It is also very important that your assumptions be realistic. If you are now earning $40,000 per year after taxes and are near the peak of your career, you should not assume a promotion with a substantial salary increase. Instead, calculate that your earnings will grow at the rate of inflation, or 5 percent per year (or less if wages in your industry have not been keeping pace with inflation). Then, when you look toward your planned retirement date, say eight years from now, you will have a more realistic income objective for your after-retirement years.

In looking through the material currently available on retirement financial planning, we have found that while there are all kinds of financial tables, charts, and forms, there are very few realistic examples to serve as a backdrop against which you can prepare your own financial plan. This book, in an effort to correct that problem, will introduce you to three fictional persons: a married couple, Mike and Doris Williams, and a single woman named Joan Stuart.

2

The Model Retirement
Net Worth Profiles

We'll start with Mike and Doris Williams. Mike is now 55 years old and Doris is 53. They live in the Northeast, where Mike has worked for the General Manufacturing Company since graduating from high school; to date, he has accumulated a total of thirty-five years of service. He started as an assistant stock clerk, was drafted into the Army for two years at the close of the Korean conflict, and then returned to General Manufacturing as a full stock clerk. After his stint in the service he took advantage of the liberal veterans' educational benefits and entered the local four-year college's evening division while continuing to work full-time. Six years later, he received his bachelor's degree in accounting. Mike rose slowly through the ranks at General Manufacturing (the company has changed ownership several times and is now a publicly owned corporation with common stock traded on the New York Stock Exchange), and he is now manager of general ledger accounting, a position he will probably retain until retirement.

Shortly after his return from the Army, Mike married Doris. They have three children, two sons, in their middle and late 20s, and a daughter who is in her early 20s and just completed college. The two boys are both married, and the older son lives with his wife and two children in Tampa, Florida, a growing area with a very moderate climate and a large population of retirees. Their daughter recently leased an apartment with a friend near her place of employment in the city where she grew up, and the younger son lives about an hour's drive from his parents' home.

Doris was a local department store clerk at the time of their marriage and continued working until her pregnancy with their first child two years later. She remained a homemaker until seven years ago, when she returned to work as a salesperson in the women's dress shop in the local shopping mall. This was necessary in order to help provide funds for college tuitions and boarding costs for the children, who also helped themselves by arranging tuition loans and taking part-time jobs.

Mike's company provides him with a full package of benefits, including a pension plan, an employee savings plan which was started fifteen years ago, and excellent medical, dental, disability, and life insurance programs. Doris receives only group medical and life insurance; she has no company-sponsored pension or employee savings plan. Both Mike and Doris are in good health and have made it a point to take complete physical examinations each year since their early 40s.

Mike's annual salary is $45,000 and Doris earns $10,000, for a combined family income of $55,000. Both Mike and Doris have been reasonably frugal and have taken advantage of savings opportunities provided by Mike's employer. They have also made other modest and conservative investments. When Mike's father died seven years ago at age 72 (his mother died at 70), Mike received an inheritance of $35,000, which he invested in a summer home and some common stocks and mutual funds. Doris's mother, now 78 years old, lives off Social Security and a small pension from her deceased husband's employer. Her husband died eighteen years ago of heart disease at age 61. She also has some modest savings and is self-sufficient.

The Williamses have recently begun to give serious thought to their future retirement. This is a natural phenomenon for new empty nesters, but in the Williams' case was prompted by the sudden closing of a local manufacturing division of a major national corporation, which consolidated operations in another city and offered jobs and relocation to only a small group of employees. One of Mike's closest friends, Bill Adams, was let go after twenty-eight years of service, at the age of 58. Six months later he still has not found a suitable position and will soon exhaust his severance benefits. His early-retirement income is clearly inadequate. Although Mike is confident that this will not happen to him,

Bill's situation has affected him deeply. In a recent letter to all employees, prompted by the closing of the manufacturing division for which Bill worked, the chairman of General Manufacturing indicated that the corporation had no plans to consolidate any of its operations, unless, of course, economic conditions should change.

Mike Williams thought hard about that letter, and about his friend Bill, and decided it was high time to do some really careful planning to determine where he was financially right now, and where he would be ten years hence, at 65, when he would probably want to retire from his present full-time position. Having created a financial plan, he felt that he could then manipulate his estimates and avoid disaster if he were given an unpleasant surprise by his employer.

Mike and Doris assembled all of their bank account, investment, employee savings plan, and loan data and began the process of retirement financial planning. The first part of this process involves the development of actual amounts and estimates for a personal balance sheet. This is called the Retirement Net Worth Profile and it enables a PREP (*Pre-REtirement Planner*) to determine current net worth or wealth and project that out to the planned retirement date, when Mike will be 65 and Doris will be 63. Here are the results:

RETIREMENT NET WORTH PROFILE, MIKE AND DORIS WILLIAMS

Assets	Today	At Retirement
1. Cash on hand in bank accounts, certificates of deposit, etc., which you can gain access to immediately, even if there is a penalty	$15,000	$15,000
2. Securities, including bonds, common and preferred stocks, government securities, mutual funds, etc.	10,000	22,000
3. Cash value of company employee investment fund or other company savings plans such as 401(k) plans, etc.	60,000	203,000

Assets	Today	At Retirement
4. Cash value of IRA accounts and Keoghs (HR 10);—Husband	12,000	26,000
Wife	9,000	19,000
5. Cash surrender values of life insurance policies	15,000	20,000
6. Value of your home	140,000	188,000
7. Value of any other real estate investments, summer houses, etc.	50,000	81,000
8. Value of your full- or part-time business	—	—
9. Value of your cars	8,000	20,000
10. Value of any collectibles, gold, jewelry, furs, etc.	5,000	8,000
Total Assets	**$324,000**	**$602,000**

Liabilities		
1. Remaining principal due on mortgages on home and any real estate investments	30,000	—
2. Balance of car loan	5,000	—
3. Balance of any bank loans, personal debt, credit cards, charge accounts, etc.	1,000	—
Total Liabilities	**$36,000**	**—**

Retirement Net Worth	$288,000	$602,000

You will notice that we have rounded all of the numbers to the nearest thousand. There really is no need to be more precise than that on the Retirement Net Worth Profile. But behind these numbers there are some details that you should understand in order to complete your own profile properly. Let's review how Mike and Doris assembled their data, starting under the heading "Assets."

The cash on hand totals $15,000 today and $15,000 at retirement. Today's balances include their joint checking account, which usually has a balance averaging $3,000; their money market savings account which has $4,000; and three certificates of deposit, one maturing in one year for $3,000, one in two years for $3,000, and one in three years for $2,000. These amounts total $15,000. For the past three years the Williamses have maintained approximately the same cash balances. They have used their interest income for occasional travel and have made no attempt to add to their cash savings. They have assumed that despite inflation averaging 5 percent for the next ten years, they will not increase their cash resources at retirement.

Securities total $10,000 and are estimated to grow to $22,000 at retirement. The Williamses have two investments: common stock in the local utility company worth $5,000 at market (200 shares at $25) as of yesterday's closing price on the New York Stock Exchange, and $5,000 in a popular mutual fund. These securities were purchased with part of Mike's inheritance seven years ago and have doubled in value since that time.

While the current value is $10,000, retirement planning requires Mike and Doris to estimate the value of these assets at retirement. This is done by assuming a rate of growth and using Table 1, The Future Value of One Dollar (see opposite page). The number of years or time periods is given in the far left-hand column and rates of growth (or yields) are read across the top, starting with 1 percent. The resulting numbers are called "interest factors" and are frequently used in retirement planning.

Doris and Mike think the value of the assets will appreciate by 8 percent annually. This is a conservative return to be achieved by price appreciation and dividend reinvestments. Once this rate has been selected, it may be used to estimate the value of these investments at retirement. Locate the interest factor for ten years at 8 percent. You will

T A B L E   1

The Future Value of One Dollar

Period	1%	2%	3%	4%	5%	6%	7%
1	1.010	1.020	1.030	1.040	1.050	1.060	1.070
2	1.020	1.040	1.061	1.082	1.102	1.124	1.145
3	1.030	1.061	1.093	1.125	1.158	1.191	1.225
4	1.041	1.082	1.126	1.170	1.216	1.262	1.311
5	1.051	1.104	1.159	1.217	1.276	1.338	1.403
6	1.062	1.126	1.194	1.265	1.340	1.419	1.501
7	1.072	1.149	1.230	1.316	1.407	1.504	1.606
8	1.083	1.172	1.267	1.369	1.477	1.594	1.718
9	1.094	1.195	1.305	1.423	1.551	1.689	1.838
10	1.105	1.219	1.344	1.480	1.629	1.791	1.967
11	1.116	1.243	1.384	1.539	1.710	1.898	2.105
12	1.127	1.268	1.426	1.601	1.796	2.012	2.252
13	1.138	1.294	1.469	1.665	1.886	2.133	2.410
14	1.149	1.319	1.513	1.732	1.980	2.261	2.579
15	1.161	1.346	1.558	1.801	2.079	2.397	2.759
16	1.173	1.373	1.605	1.873	2.183	2.540	2.952
17	1.184	1.400	1.653	1.948	2.292	2.693	3.159
18	1.196	1.428	1.702	2.026	2.407	2.854	3.380
19	1.208	1.457	1.754	2.107	2.527	3.026	3.617
20	1.220	1.486	1.806	2.191	2.653	3.207	3.870
25	1.282	1.641	2.094	2.666	3.386	4.292	5.427
30	1.348	1.811	2.427	3.243	4.322	5.743	7.612

Period	8%	9%	10%	12%	14%	15%	16%
1	1.080	1.090	1.100	1.120	1.140	1.150	1.160
2	1.166	1.188	1.210	1.254	1.300	1.322	1.346
3	1.260	1.295	1.331	1.405	1.482	1.521	1.561
4	1.360	1.412	1.464	1.574	1.689	1.749	1.811
5	1.469	1.539	1.611	1.762	1.925	2.011	2.100
6	1.587	1.677	1.772	1.974	2.195	2.313	2.436
7	1.714	1.828	1.949	2.211	2.502	2.660	2.826
8	1.851	1.993	2.144	2.476	2.853	3.059	3.278
9	1.999	2.172	2.358	2.773	3.252	3.518	3.803
10	2.159	2.367	2.594	3.106	3.707	4.046	4.411
11	2.332	2.580	2.853	3.479	4.226	4.652	5.117
12	2.518	2.813	3.138	3.896	4.818	5.350	5.936
13	2.720	3.066	3.452	4.363	5.492	6.153	6.886
14	2.937	3.342	3.797	4.887	6.261	7.076	7.988
15	3.172	3.642	4.177	5.474	7.138	8.137	9.266
16	3.426	3.970	4.595	6.130	8.137	9.358	10.748
17	3.700	4.328	5.054	6.866	9.276	10.761	12.468
18	3.996	4.717	5.560	7.690	10.575	12.375	14.463
19	4.316	5.142	6.116	8.613	12.056	14.232	16.777
20	4.661	5.604	6.728	9.646	13.743	16.367	19.461
25	6.848	8.623	10.835	17.000	26.462	32.919	40.874
30	10.063	13.268	17.449	29.960	50.950	66.212	85.850

note that the factor for 8 percent over ten years is 2.159. Multiply that factor by the $10,000 current value of the securities investments and the result is $21,590, which was rounded up to $22,000.

Notice one difference in the ''Today'' and ''At Retirement'' columns for cash and for securities. There is absolutely no growth planned for Mike and Doris's cash balances in retirement. This is worth thinking about for a moment. They intend to maintain a modest cash reserve for immediate emergencies or other cash needs, and the current and projected amounts are the same. Mike and Doris realize that cash balances are not where money is made. For their securities investments, however, they expect a return that is greater than the rate of inflation; and in a period of just ten years, at a conservative 8 percent, those investments are expected to more than double—from $10,000 to $22,000!

Mike is very fortunate to have a company employee investment fund available for retirement savings. Most large and medium-size companies offer similar programs, but unfortunately some *Pre-REtirement Planners* will not have the advantage of this type of program. Joan Stuart, our alternate case study, does not share in such a fund, and as you will see, this hole in her personal portfolio will have a dramatic impact on her ability to achieve her retirement objective.

At the present time, Mike's employee investment plan is worth $60,000. A value of $58,000 was shown on the last quarterly statement Mike received. He brought that up to date by adding his contributions since the statement date, adding the company's matching-funds contribution of its common stock and estimating the interest income applicable to the period (three months), and then rounding to the nearest $1,000. The company's matching contribution, in Mike's case, is about one-third of his contribution: he contributes $3,000 per year and the company adds another $1,000. The fund is managed conservatively, as most company funds are, and has earned an average return of about 10 percent over the past several years.

The Williamses gave considerable thought to their at-retirement estimate for Mike's employee investment plan before committing a figure to paper. Mike has ten more years of contributions ahead of him, and he has no intention of contributing more than $3,000 per year, although the plan permits employee contributions up to $4,000. His contribution, together with the company's matching contribution of

$1,000 (it's referred to as a matching contribution because a participant can contribute as little as $500 per year and the company will match that contribution and will do so up to $1,000), adds up to $4,000 per year. While the plan has been earning an average of 10 percent annually, including increases in the value of the common stock together with dividends, the Williamses decided to assume a slightly slower rate of growth for the next ten years.

At 9 percent per year over ten years, the present $60,000 will grow to $142,000. Make the calculation yourself from Table 1. That's right! The number of years is ten, and rate is 9 percent, so the calculation is $60,000 × 2.367, which equals approximately $142,000. The $142,000 does not consider any additional contributions. Mike expects to invest an additional $4,000 (his $3,000 plus the company's $1,000). How much will these contributions be worth after ten years? The answer is found by using Table 2 (see page 14), which gives the future value of a series of payments (i.e., an annuity table). The interest factors on this table represent the future value of one dollar invested each period (such as each year) at the given rate of growth or yield. The interest factor for ten years at 9 percent is 15.193. Multiply $4,000 per year × 15.193 and the result is $60,772, which was rounded to $61,000.

The total of $203,000 ($142,000 + $61,000) is the cash value of the company investment fund at retirement. A rather nice nest egg, resulting, really, from a relatively painless way to save for the future.

Next come the IRA accounts. (Another retirement plan, called a Keogh or HR 10, is available for the self-employed.) The Williamses, who are not eligible for Keoghs, could take tax-deductible IRA contributions until the 1987 federal tax law came into effect. Their present account balances are $12,000 for Mike and $9,000 for Doris. They made their last contributions in 1986 for that year and have no intention of contributing further because they can no longer obtain a tax deduction on their contributions. These funds are managed by a local bank, which has invested them in U.S. Treasury instruments of various types that have yielded about 8 percent growth per year and are expected to grow at about the same rate over the next ten years. The ''At Retirement'' values come from applying Table 1's factor for 8% over ten years, which is 2.159. Both accounts will more than double, to $26,000 ($12,000 × 2.159) and $19,000 ($9,000 × 2.159) over the ten-year period.

T A B L E   2

The Future Value of an Annuity of One Dollar for N Periods

Period	1%	2%	3%	4%	5%	6%
1	1.000	1.000	1.000	1.000	1.000	1.000
2	2.010	2.020	2.030	2.040	2.050	2.060
3	3.030	3.060	3.091	3.122	3.152	3.184
4	4.060	4.122	4.184	4.246	4.310	4.375
5	5.101	5.204	5.309	5.416	5.526	5.637
6	6.152	6.308	6.468	6.633	6.802	6.975
7	7.214	7.434	7.662	7.898	8.142	8.394
8	8.286	8.583	8.892	9.214	9.549	9.897
9	9.369	9.755	10.159	10.583	11.027	11.491
10	10.462	10.950	11.464	12.006	12.578	13.181
11	11.567	12.169	12.808	13.486	14.207	14.972
12	12.683	13.412	14.192	15.026	15.917	16.870
13	13.809	14.680	15.618	16.627	17.713	18.882
14	14.947	15.974	17.086	18.292	19.599	21.051
15	16.097	17.293	18.599	20.024	21.579	23.276
16	17.258	18.639	20.157	21.825	23.657	25.673
17	18.430	20.012	21.762	23.698	25.840	28.213
18	19.615	21.412	23.414	25.645	28.132	30.906
19	20.811	22.841	25.117	27.671	30.539	33.760
20	22.019	24.297	26.870	29.778	33.066	36.786
25	28.243	32.030	36.459	41.646	47.727	54.865
30	34.785	40.568	47.575	56.085	66.439	79.058

Period	7%	8%	9%	10%	12%	14%
1	1.000	1.000	1.000	1.000	1.000	1.000
2	2.070	2.080	2.090	2.100	2.120	2.140
3	3.215	3.246	3.278	3.310	3.374	3.440
4	4.440	4.506	4.573	4.641	4.770	4.921
5	5.751	5.867	5.985	6.105	6.353	6.610
6	7.153	7.336	7.523	7.716	8.115	8.536
7	8.654	8.923	9.200	9.487	10.089	10.730
8	10.260	10.637	11.028	11.436	12.300	13.233
9	11.978	12.488	13.021	13.579	14.776	16.085
10	13.816	14.487	15.193	15.937	17.549	19.337
11	15.784	16.645	17.560	18.531	20.655	23.044
12	17.888	18.977	20.141	21.384	24.138	27.271
13	20.141	21.495	22.953	24.523	28.029	32.089
14	22.550	24.215	26.019	27.975	32.393	37.581
15	25.129	27.152	29.361	31.772	37.280	43.842
16	27.888	30.324	33.003	35.950	42.753	50.980
17	30.840	33.750	36.974	40.545	48.884	59.118
18	33.999	37.450	41.301	45.599	55.750	68.394
19	37.379	41.446	46.018	51.159	63.440	78.969
20	40.995	45.762	51.160	57.275	72.052	91.025
25	63.249	73.106	84.701	98.347	133.334	181.871
30	94.461	113.283	136.308	164.494	241.333	356.787

Both Mike and Doris have group term life insurance. Mike is well protected at three times his base salary, and Doris has a modest $8,000 policy through her employer. Neither plan has any cash value and both are fully paid by their employers. Mike did take out an individual life insurance policy, which will be fully paid up at age 65. This was done shortly after the birth of their first child, and the cash (or loan) value of this policy is now $15,000. This will grow to $20,000 at age 65, according to Mike's insurance agent. The death benefit, of course, will still be $30,000, but for loan purposes only $20,000 can be obtained. The cash value represents the true value of the insurance policy to the Williamses when Mike retires, as planned, at 65.

The Williamses estimate the present value of their home at $140,000. Be conservative in estimating the value of your home. We all feel that the place where we live is worth more than the value put on it by the marketplace. The Williamses asked a local real estate agent to estimate the price of their property based on a quick sale (within thirty days). Maybe they could get another $5,000 or $7,000 if they decide to sell. Although, as you will see shortly, they have no need or desire to move from their present neighborhood, if their retirement planning requires they sell and if they have assigned a reasonable value to their house, they will not be in for a rude shock when they put it on the market.

The Williamses decided to take a conservative approach to the future value of this property. They don't believe that the rate of growth in the value of their home will achieve the average inflation rate of 5 percent. They have settled on 3 percent annually as a conservative estimate applied on the current value, which has increased sharply over the past few years. Three percent might be too conservative but Doris and Mike would rather err on the side of conservatism than inflate the value of their assets at retirement. They are being careful to avoid planning errors that may be recognized too late to correct them. Again, using Table 1, the estimated value of their home in ten years at a growth rate of 3 percent is $188,000 ($140,000 × 1.344 = $188,160), rounded to the nearest $1,000

Mike and Doris are fortunate to own a summer home; it is free and clear of any mortgages, because Mike put most of his inheritance from his father into this weekend retreat in the lake country, about a two-hour drive from their home. It turned out to be a wonderful investment, appreciating from the original price of $25,000 to a conservative $50,000 today. That's an average growth rate of about 10 percent since the original purchase seven years ago. Because the demand for summer places is a little stronger than the demand for houses in the Williams' year-round neighborhood, they decided that the value of their summer house will increase at about 5 percent per year, parallel with inflation, and it will be worth $81,000 at retirement. (See if you get $81,000. Remember to use Table 1, The Future Value of One Dollar.)

The value of your cars is a necessary entry on your personal Retirement Net Worth Profile for two reasons. First, you must plan to assure that you have a family car of appropriate size, preferably a new one, at the time of your retirement. Second, you may have to consider reducing the quality of your car to cut repair bills and operating expenses, so that you can achieve your retirement income objectives. The Williamses have maintained a modest midsize car, trading it in every five years or so. Their current car is worth $8,000, based on advertisements in the local paper for the same year and model. They plan to replace this car on a schedule that will result in their purchase of a new car for cash just before Mike's retirement. They would like to buy a car identical to the one they now have, which currently costs $12,000 new. Assuming a projected increase of 5 percent per year, a new car will cost $20,000 in ten years.

Mike and Doris also own some collectibles which could be sold to raise funds for their retirement if they wished. These kinds of assets— jewelry, furs, art, and rare books—should be listed in your Retirement Net Worth Profile. It is unwise to include household furnishings, sofas, and dining-room sets, however, *unless* you plan to finance part of your retirement through the sale of valuable antiques or other furnishings that are not needed to outfit your retirement living quarters.

The Williamses elected to include only their collectibles, which would be expendable if it meant maintaining the quality of their retirement. These collectibles are currently valued at $5,000, based on the purchase prices offered by local dealers. The "At Retirement" value was assumed to reflect the rate of inflation of 5 percent per year, thus resulting in a total projection of $8,000 ($5,000 $\times$ 1.629 = $8,145).

The current value of the Williams' total assets is $324,000. Ten years from now, using reasonable, conservative estimates, these same assets will have grown to $602,000. This growth may strike you as unbelievably optimistic, but it really isn't. In virtually every instance the

Williamses used growth rates to forecast that were lower than have actually been experienced over the past several years.

Now let's take a look at Mike and Doris's liabilities. First of all, their biggest liability is their home mortgage. The Williamses purchased their current home when Mike was 44, and they took a twenty-year mortgage because they wanted to be sure their home was free and clear by the time Mike was 65. They still owe $30,000 of principal, but it will be fully paid, or "amortized," at retirement.

Their car loan is their second-largest debt. Because they no longer contribute to their IRA accounts or pay their children's education expenses, they are now in a position to pay cash for a new car, after the value of the trade-in. Therefore they plan to have no car-loan debt by the time Mike reaches 65.

The Williamses currently have some modest credit card debt, which is being paid on an installment basis. They also use a national credit card for a variety of purchases and occasional restaurant charges, but the monthly bill is fully paid when it is received. The credit card balance will be fully paid over the next year or so, and the Williamses do not foresee using any form of installment debt beyond that point.

We have completed Mike and Doris Williams's Retirement Net Worth Profile. Their current worth is $288,000, and their net worth at retirement, assuming everything proceeds according to plan, will total $602,000. But what if everything does not proceed according to plan? Once each year, preferably right after filling out their annual federal income tax returns, Mike and Doris plan to sit back and rethink their assumptions for their Retirement Net Worth Profile. You should do the same. It means gathering all the data again, looking at the latest balances versus a year ago, and examining the inflation-rate and growth-rate assumptions. If the assumptions made last year have not changed significantly, put the papers away until next year. But if they have changed, then make the necessary revisions.

The Retirement Net Worth Profile is the basis for the Retirement Income Profile that follows. Your retirement net worth is a major factor for determining your retirement income. It is therefore of critical importance that you realistically value your assets and recognize all of your liabilities so that you do not subsequently overstate retirement income.

We talked a little earlier about allowing for the impact of unplanned events on our retirement financial estimates. Let's assume that General

Manufacturing is having difficulties in strongly competitive markets. The corporation has had to adjust prices to meet competition from more efficient foreign manufacturers. As a result, it may consolidate certain plant activities at its divisional headquarters in a city in the Midwest. This includes some plant accounting, purchasing, and personnel activities. Mike believes that by age 61 his job may be eliminated. The company, trying to be as fair as possible, then will offer Mike the opportunity to stay on for six months, help with the consolidation, and take early retirement at age 62, under provisions of the company retirement plan. Mike will also receive severance pay of one week for each year of service, or forty-two weeks of salary plus three weeks of vacation severance, for a total of forty-five weeks. His salary at the time of his severance from General Manufacturing will be $63,000 per year, and his severance date is November 30.

What will the Williams' Retirement Net Worth Profile look like with Mike at age 62 and Doris at age 60? The estimates for age 62 are obtained in the same way as for age 65, except the number of years is seven, which requires using different interest factors. The age 62 and age 65 forecasts are as follows:

RETIREMENT NET WORTH PROFILE, MIKE AND DORIS WILLIAMS

Assets	At Retirement Age 65	Age 62
1. Cash on hand and in bank accounts, certificates of deposit, etc., which you can gain access to immediately, even if there is a penalty	$ 15,000	$ 18,000
1a. After-tax value of 45 weeks' severance pay	—	44,000
2. Securities, including bonds, common and preferred stocks, government securities, mutual funds, etc.	22,000	17,000

Assets	At Retirement	
	Age 65	Age 62
3. Cash value of company employee investment fund or other company savings plans such as 401(k) plans, etc.	203,000	147,000
4. Cash value of IRA accounts and Keoghs (HR 10): Husband:	26,000	21,000
Wife:	19,000	15,000
5. Cash surrender values of life insurance policies	20,000	18,000
6. Value of your home	188,000	172,000
7. Value of any other real estate investments, summer houses, etc	81,000	70,000
8. Value of your full-or part-time business	—	—
9. Value of your cars	20,000	14,000
10. Values of any collectibles, gold, jewelry, furs, etc.	8,000	7,000
Total Assets	602,000	543,000

Liabilities		
1. Remaining principal due on mortgages on your home and any real estate investments	—	$ 10,000
2. Balance of car loan	—	6,000
3. Balance of any bank loans, personal debt, credit cards, charge accounts, etc.	—	—
Total Liabilities	—	$ 16,000
Retirement Net Worth	$602,000	$527,000

The Williams' estimated retirement net worth *declines* by $75,000 because of the earlier retirement. Note that under "Assets," cash balances are actually $3,000 *higher* than at age 65. That's because the Williamses were saving to purchase their next car at normal retirement (65) for cash, after trade-in of their four-year-old car. The major addition to cash is the after-tax value of forty-five weeks of severance pay. The entire amount is paid on November 30 and hence is subject to maximum federal and state income taxes. The remaining values at age 62 reflect the same assumptions used for age 65, adjusted for the reduction of three years.

Now let's look at Joan Stuart's situation, which involves an entirely different set of problems and possible solutions. Joan has lived in the same major Northwestern city all of her life, except for her four undergraduate years at the University of Southern California. Joan majored in English in college, and after trying several administrative and retail sales clerk positions she settled in as an assistant office manager for a regional, privately owned building supply organization, Northwestern Building Supplies, Inc. That was twenty-four years ago, when Joan was 29. She was married briefly while in her mid-20s, but was divorced two years later and never remarried. Now 53, she lives alone, maintaining a small circle of single friends.

Ms. Stuart is presently the office manager for the local branch of Northwestern Building Supplies. She is highly regarded by her employer; the company is still privately owned and is managed by third-generation descendants of the original owners. About ten years ago, the company introduced a pension plan for all employees. It is a modest plan which will provide Joan Stuart with payments equivalent to 40 percent of her final salary at age 65. The plan also provides for reduced payments of 5 percent for each year of early retirement to age 55, as well as paid medical insurance and group life insurance with a face value equal to annual salary. The company does not offer any other savings alternatives such as U.S. savings bonds or payroll deduction plans.

Ms. Stuart now earns $30,000 per year and can expect annual increases at about the rate of inflation. She saves approximately 5 percent of her after-tax income. She has never opened an IRA account. Joan lives in a small one-bedroom rental apartment, ten minutes by car from her office. She currently pays $500 per month rent, plus utilities, and is in the last year of a two-year lease.

One of Joan's best friends has an older sister who recently retired from her local company. She had a similar retirement income program and is also single. She found it difficult to make ends meet in retirement and was forced to make some adjustments in her lifestyle. Joan is concerned that she may be faced with the same problem when she reaches retirement age. Thus she is determined that she'll plan now to avoid a possible problem when it's too late to do anything about it. Here is Joan's Retirement Net Worth Profile:

RETIREMENT NET WORTH PROFILE, JOAN STUART

Assets	Today	At Retirement
1. Cash on hand and in bank accounts, certificates of deposit, etc., which she can gain access to immediately, even if there is a penalty	$20,000	$68,000
2. Securities, including bonds, common and preferred stocks, government securities, mutual funds, etc.	—	—
3. Cash value of company employee investment fund or other company savings plans such as 401(k) plans, etc.	—	—
4. Cash value of IRA accounts and Keoghs (HR 10)	—	—
5. Cash surrender values of life insurance policies	3,000	5,000
6. Value of home	—	—
7. Value of any other real estate investments, summer houses, etc.	—	—

Assets	Today	At Retirement
8. Value of full- or part-time business	—	—
9. Value of car	6,000	9,000
10. Values of any collectibles, gold, jewelry, furs, etc.	3,000	5,000
Total Assets	**$35,000**	**$87,000**

Liabilities		
1. Remaining principal due on mortgages on home and any real estate investments	—	—
2. Balance of car loan:	$ 3,000	$ 4,000
3. Balance of any bank loans, personal debt, credit cards, charge accounts, etc.	1,000	None
Total Liabilities	**$ 4,000**	**$ 4,000**
Retirement Net Worth	**$26,000**	**$83,000**

Look back on pages 8 and 9 and compare Joan Stuart's Retirement Net Worth Profile with Mike and Doris Williams's. We are looking at two different worlds, two distinct life-styles. The Williamses have had the opportunity to build wealth through payroll savings and real estate. Although Joan Stuart's opportunities have been more limited, she has not taken advantage of those available to her.

Let's take a look at where Joan believes she will be financially at age 65. First, like many others she has been reasonably prudent in assuring that she builds savings. She has been conservative, keeping all of her excess funds in passbook savings and certificates of deposit. Today she is earning an average yield of about 7 percent from these savings. Joan believes she will average about 6 percent interest on these savings over the next 12 years until her retirement. Joan is very careful to save about 5 percent of her weekly take-home pay, and this will also earn interest at an average of 6 percent. As a result, her cash savings will increase by a healthy margin owing to systematic savings and reasonably conservative earnings on all of her savings. By age 65, Joan will have more than tripled her current savings of $20,000 to $68,000.

Sadly, once we get past her savings, Joan has few assets that can contribute to her retirement. She owns no real estate. Her personal Life Insurance policy has a face value of $7,000. To make matters worse, her company-paid health and life insurance plans terminate at retirement.

Joan maintains a popular compact car and trades it in every five or six years. She has a small amount of jewelry, which she would be willing to sell to help finance her retirement.

Her total assets of $35,000 will grow to $87,000 by age 65. Her liabilities are also modest, consisting of her sixty-month installment car loan and an installment credit card which she intends to pay off fully over the next two years.

Joan's Retirement Net Worth Profile is a very modest $26,000 today and will increase to an inadequate $83,000 at her anticipated retirement date, twelve years from now.

In the event that she suddenly finds herself without a job before she reaches retirement age, her assets may shrink, as she uses them to sustain herself while looking for employment.

We have spent a fair amount of time now determining and forecasting net worth at retirement. We have done so because the Retirement Net Worth Profile provides a thorough estimate of the resources you can apply to your retirement years. These assets will be needed at an increasing rate as your age increases. This will be demonstrated in chapter 3 when we build the retirement income profiles for the Williamses and Joan Stuart.

3

The Model Retirement Expense and Income Profiles

Once we have an estimate of our net worth at retirement, we can develop Retirement Expense and Income Profiles. Our objective is to determine what our income will be when we retire. We will focus first on what our retirement income will be in year 1 of retirement, and then project these estimates over the full span of our retirement years. We are going to look ahead twenty-five years from age 65 for both Mike Williams and Joan Stuart. Both Joan Stuart and Doris Williams, at age 63, have longer life expectancies than Mike, but in order to minimize the complexity of these examples, we'll assume the same retirement period for all three. We suggest you use at least twenty-five years from age 65 for your planning (or twenty-eight years from age 62, if that's your preferred retirement age). Although the odds are against your living to be 90, you want to make sure there's something in the kitty in case you defy the actuarial tables.

We will need to prepare two profiles, a Cash Expense Profile and a Cash Income Profile, and compare the results to determine whether there is an income deficiency during retirement. While it is important that we continue to use realistic and conservative estimates, it is especially critical that the results of this planning effort mean *taking action now* to correct potentially serious retirement income deficiencies in the future. We'll continue with our two case studies, starting with Mike and Doris Williams.

CASH EXPENSE PROFILE, MIKE AND DORIS WILLIAMS

	Today	At Retirement
A. Housing Expenses		
1. Mortgage	$4,700	—
2. Real estate taxes—principal home	3,500	5,700
3. Real estate taxes—summer home	2,000	3,200
4. Utilities	2,500	4,100
5. Maintenance and repairs	2,800	4,600
6. Insurance	1,300	2,200
Total housing expenses	$16,800	$19,800
B. Food and Personal Expenses		
1. Dining at home	5,000	7,500
2. Dining out	1,200	2,600
3. Personal care	600	1,000
4. Clothing	1,500	2,100
5. Recreation	1,000	2,000
6. Furniture, appliances, etc.	1,000	1,600
7. All other	1,000	1,600
Total food and personal expenses	$11,300	$18,400

	Today	At Retirement
C. Automobile Expenses		
1. Loan payments, or savings to replace auto	2,000	3,300
2. Fuel, maintenance, and repairs	1,400	2,300
3. Insurance	600	1,000
Total automobile expenses	$4,000	6,600
D. Travel expenses	4,000	8,000
E. Life insurance—paid-up at age 65	500	—
F. Medical, dental, and accident insurance	—	2,300
G. Gifts and contributions	1,500	2,400
TOTAL CASH EXPENSES	$38,100	$57,500

The Cash Expense Profile indicates that the Williamses currently spend $38,100 annually. Doris and Mike were able to determine the total rather easily because they pay bills by check and draw checks for cash from the same checking account. They simply added all checks written during the year, using twelve monthly bank statement totals. They could also have added up the checks entered in their checkbook for the twelve-month period with substantially the same results, although it would have taken longer to do it that way.

Doris and Mike then determined the major types of expenses and entered them in the Cash Expense Profile. While we have included considerable detail in this example, you might want to make a quick estimate by determining the total first, then substracting any spending you won't have at retirement. If the Williamses did this, they would have subtracted the mortgage payments (because their mortgage is fully paid by retirement) as well as the current life insurance premiums for the paid-up-at-age-65 policy. The resulting balance would then have been estimated at retirement by increasing it at the 5 percent annual rate of inflation. As we already know, this means applying the interest factor of 1.629 from Table 1, The Future Value of One Dollar, in the previous chapter to the balance to determine the amount at retirement.

The Williamses would then make two adjustments. First, they would add $1,500 to provide for air fare and expenses for two additional trips they plan to make to Tampa, Florida, to visit their older son and his family. Given their additional leisure time, most retirees travel more, even if only on local day trips. Second, they would add the cost of supplemental health and medical insurance to assure adequate total medical insurance coverage during the retirement years. Keep in mind that these estimates are *at retirement* and reflect current expense increases for inflation of 5 percent per year.

Let's now put all of this together in a table that illustrates how the "quick" cash expenditure estimate works:

	Today	At Retirement
Total expenses per checking account data		
	$38,100	
Less: Mortgage payments	4,700	
Life insurance premiums	500	
Net expenses applicable to retirement	$32,900	
Growth at 5% per year for 10 years	× 1.629	
Expenses at retirement		$53,700
Additional travel expenses		1,500
Supplemental medical insurance		2,300
Total cash expenses at retirement		$57,500

Notice this is the same amount determined earlier when all the expenses were enumerated and added. This method is only a "first pass" estimate. It is especially applicable to you *Pre-REtirement Planners* who are looking for a quick way to determine if you're on track. We suggest that all individuals planning for retirement take the time to determine what you are spending your money on. Besides being revealing, it may well provide you with the information you need to adjust your spending habits and thus ensure your financial independence at retirement.

The Williamses were very careful with their estimates, because they wanted to be sure they had the funds necessary to enjoy their retirement. For example, while total food and personal expenses were planned to increase at the rate of inflation, Mike and Doris knew they would be spending their money a little differently. They felt they would be dining out more, and while they would spend relatively less on clothing, they would spend more on recreation.

The Williamses are going to do everything possible to maintain the same life-style in retirement as they enjoyed before retirement. Their Cash Expense Profile provides for this life-style. The question to be answered is this: does their Retirement Income Profile enable them to afford their pre-retirement life-style? The answer is *almost* yes, as the following *Cash Income Profile* will show:

CASH INCOME PROFILE, MIKE AND DORIS WILLIAMS

	Today	At Retirement
A. From today to retirement		
1. Net income from salaries and wages after all tax and other deductions	$37,000	$59,900
2. Interest received from savings accounts, certificates of deposit, etc.	900	900
3. Dividends received from investments in securities	800	1,800

	Today	At Retirement
4. Other income	—	—
5. Less estimated federal, state, and local taxes on items 2–4 above	(600)	(1,000)
Total cash income from today to retirement	**$38,100**	**$61,600**

B. Cash income after retirement

   1. Retirement income

a. Social Security (½ taxable)	$25,200
b. Company pension plan (all taxable)	32,500
2. Interest and dividends from A2 and A3	2,700
3. Other income from A4, if applicable	—
4. Less federal, state, and local taxes on all of the above	(6,800)
Cash income before use of other assets	**$53,600**

Less: cash expenses at retirement from Cash Expense Profile	57,500

Mike and Doris almost have enough income without liquidating some of their assets! They are only $3,900 short, which they can meet by selling some of their stock:

Additional after-tax income required to meet cash expenses at retirement	$ 3,900

	Today	At Retirement
C. Sources of additional after-tax income		
1. Proceeds from sale of securities, after $100 sales commission		4,400
2. Less federal, state, and local taxes on sale of securities		(500)
Total additional after-tax income		$3,900

The Williamses are indeed in good financial condition for their *first* year of retirement. They are able to meet their cash expenses at retirement by using only $4,500 ($3,900 after tax) in funds from their securities investments.

Let's review the cash income form carefully. Section A of the form, ''From today to retirement,'' is necessary for assuring that you review, and make a decision on, each element of your current income. Some will grow with inflation, such as dividend income; others, such as salary, will be replaced by other forms of income (pension); and still others will continue into retirement, such as interest income.

Line A1 is the net income (after all tax, insurance, and employee savings deductions) from the salary and wages of Mike and Doris. Today's income has been projected to grow at 5 percent per year, as we previously discussed. The ''At Retirement'' estimate is the last full year's net salary and wages income for the Williamses before their retirement. Lines A2 through A4 include all other forms of income the Williamses currently use to maintain their life-style, less, on line A5, the income taxes they pay on such other income. At the time of their retirement the Williamses will enjoy a total cash income of $61,600. In their first year of retirement their total cash income will be $53,600. Their total income is reduced because their income from Social Security and the company pension plan is less than their former net income from salaries and wages. However, the Williams' retirement income objective is also lower. That objective is the total of their Cash Expense Profile at retirement, $57,500. This is the amount required to maintain exactly the same life-style that requires $61,600 just prior to retirement.

The entries in section B, "Cash income after retirement," reflect the income Mike and Doris will actually receive after retirement from Social Security, Mike's company pension plan, and their continued interest and dividend income. These are the elements of income that are reasonably certain.

The Social Security income reflects Mike's payments, which are at the maximum because he has met the Social Security requirements for maximum payments. Doris has also retired and is receiving payments as Mike's spouse, but at a reduced rate, because she started collecting at age 63.

Mike's retirement income from General Manufacturing is based on his final annual salary. Keep in mind that Mike and Doris are doing their pre-retirement projections ten years before their planned retirement. They have estimated Mike's final salary based on annual increases of 5 percent, equivalent to the assumed annual rate of inflation. Company pension plans usually offer several options for pension income. These include single and joint life annuities which are payable over the retiree's life only (single), or the retiree's and spouse's lives (joint). There are also annuities for a guaranteed number of years, such as ten or fifteen. If the retiree dies, the beneficiary or the beneficiary's estate continues to receive the same payment until the period expires. Mike and Doris decided to take the "joint and ⅔ survivor annuity," which pays $32,500 per year (50 percent of Mike's final salary), and should either of them die, is reduced by one-third, to $21,667 per year. You should learn what choices your pension plan offers and ask your employer for estimates of benefits under the various options.

The Williamses could have selected another payment option. For example, a popular option involves joint payments that continue for the survivor at the same amount. This is called a "joint and full survivor" annuity, and it pays about 10 percent less than the joint and ⅔ survivor annuity, because the amount does not decline with the death of one spouse. Mike and Doris agonized over which option to select and decided that since Mike was in such excellent physical condition, they would risk the joint and ⅔ survivor annuity option, which gives them larger benefits now but runs the risk of lower benefits later.

Your planning should take into account your personal needs vis-à-vis your company's pension plan and alternatives, the size of your retirement net worth, and the nature of its various elements. If Mike were to die suddenly, shortly after retirement, Doris would receive an immediate reduction of $10,833 in retirement income. But she would also receive the $30,000 face value of Mike's life insurance, which is free of income taxes, and would still have all of the remaining assets available for her retirement income.

Let's assume that Mike's health deteriorates to the point where his life expectancy must be assumed to be shorter than average at the time he reaches his planned retirement age of 65. In that case he will probably select at retirement another alternative that will offer Doris more protection. The difference in retirement income would be made up by using more of the other assets the Williamses have available. Remember: *our objective is to maintain our pre-retirement standard of living.* For that reason, we're not considering any cutbacks in spending here.

Line B2 includes the interest and dividend income from the Williamses' portfolio of stocks and mutual funds. Because the Williamses have no other sources of income, there is no entry in line B3. Line B4 reflects the calculation of federal, state and local income taxes applicable to the various elements of income. State and local taxes are expected to remain at the current rate of 5 percent of gross income. (While the Williamses' state taxes retirement income, many do not, and you should check your state's requirements before doing your projections.) Federal tax rates are assumed to stay at the levels in effect in 1988, but it is assumed that the income brackets for applying such rates will grow with inflation at 5 percent per year. As a result, the first tax bracket of 15 percent for joint taxable income of 0 to $29,750 increases to 0 to $48,450 after the ten years. This could be optimistic, but the Williamses believe that the federal government will honor its promise to protect tax rates from the impact of inflation. It is also assumed that the personal exemption of $1,950 each for Mike and Doris in 1988 will increase at the rate of inflation. These factors protect Mike and Doris's retirement income from any increases in tax rates. In doing your planning, you should reconsider these assumptions in the light of the federal government's current position on personal income tax rates. You should also continue to monitor your state and local government tax requirements.

The total of B1 through B4 represents the cash income the Williamses will realize from their retirement income sources, plus their income from interest and dividends. When this total is compared with total cash expenses at retirement from pages 34 and 35, there is a *deficiency* of $3,900 in retirement income which must be covered from other sources or sale of assets. In the case of Mike and Doris, there are several sources, including securities, the company employee investment fund, and IRA accounts listed in their Retirement Net Worth Profile on pages 8 and 9.

The Williamses decided that their preferred source for this initial deficiency in retirement income would be their securities investments. These are valued at $22,000 at retirement. They considered withdrawing money from Mike's employee investment fund, which is valued at $203,000 at retirement. However, these funds are expected to earn income at 9 percent per year and are fully tax-deferred under present tax laws, as are the balances in both Mike's and Doris's IRA account.

It is better to allow funds in tax-deferred accounts to continue to increase in value as long as possible while those assets that produce currently taxable income are sold to cover any deficiency in retirement income. The advantage of that strategy may be seen in a simple example. Suppose you have $10,000 invested in a tax-deferred IRA that is earning 8 percent per year. Let's also assume that you have a $10,000 investment in a public utility common stock that is also yielding 8 percent per year, and you reinvest each year's earnings and dividends *after applicable taxes*. If your tax rate is 20 percent, how will these investments grow?

	Taxable	Tax-Deferred
	Investment	IRA
Initial value	$10,000	$10,000
Value five years from today	13,600	14,700
Value ten years from today	18,600	21,600

The reason for the higher IRA balance is that current income taxes on the 8 percent annual income are avoided. Of course, when you begin to withdraw funds from the IRA, you must pay applicable income taxes on the withdrawals. Only capital gains will be taxed when you sell your public utility stock.

As you will see a little later in this chapter, the Williamses exhaust the balance in their securities investments within a few years of retirement and will have to use the balance in Mike's employee investment fund. Of course, under current federal income tax laws, Mike must begin to withdraw funds from his employee investment fund and his IRA account when he reaches age 70½.

Now let's look at how the Williamses will cope with forced early retirement. Back on pages 18 and 19 we reviewed an early retirement scenario that resulted in a new Retirement Net Worth Profile. The next two profiles compare the effect of this early retirement on both expenses and income:

CASH EXPENSE PROFILE, MIKE AND DORIS WILLIAMS

	At Retirement	
	Age 65	Age 62
A. Housing expenses		
1. Mortgage	—	$4,700
2. Real estate taxes—principal home	$5,700	4,900
3. Real estate taxes—summer home	3,200	2,800
4. Utilities	4,100	3,500
5. Maintenance and repairs	4,600	3,900
6. Insurance	2,200	1,800
Total housing expenses	$19,800	$21,600
B. Food and personal expenses		
1. Dining at home	7,500	7,100
2. Dining out	2,600	1,700
3. Personal care	1,000	800

	At Retirement	
	Age 65	Age 62
4. Clothing	2,100	2,100
5. Recreation	2,000	1,400
6. Furniture, appliances, etc.	1,600	1,400
7. All other	1,600	1,400
Total food and personal expenses	$18,400	$15,900
C. Automobile expenses		
1. Loan payments, or savings to replace auto	3,300	2,800
2. Fuel, maintenance, and repairs	2,300	2,000
3. Insurance	1,000	800
Total automobile expenses	$6,600	$5,600
D. Travel expenses	8,000	7,100
E. Life insurance—paid-up at age 65	—	500
F. Medical, dental, and accident insurance	2,300	1,900
G. Gifts and contributions	2,400	2,100
Total Cash Expenses	$57,500	$54,700

CASH INCOME PROFILE, MIKE AND DORIS WILLIAMS

	At Retirement	
	Age 65	Age 62
A. From today to retirement		
1. Net income from salaries and wages after all tax and other deductions	$59,900	$51,800

	At Retirement	
	Age 65	Age 62
2. Interest received from savings accounts, certificates of deposit, etc.	900	900
3. Dividends received from investments in securities	1,800	1,400
4. Other income	—	—
5. Less estimated federal, state and local taxes on items 2–4 above	(1,000)	(800)
Total cash income from today to retirement	**$61,600**	**$53,500**

B. Cash income after retirement

   1. Retirement income:

a. Social Security (½ taxable)	$25,200	$14,100
b. Company pension plan (all taxable)	32,500	28,600
2. Interest and dividends from A2 and A3	2,700	2,300
3. Other income from A4, if applicable	—	—
4. Less federal, state, and local taxes on all of the above	(6,800)	(4,800)
Cash income before use of other assets	**$53,600**	**$40,200**
Less: cash expenses at retirement from Cash Expense Profile	**$57,500**	**$54,700**
Additional after-tax income required to meet cash expenses at retirement	3,900	14,500

C. Sources of additional after-tax income

1. Proceeds from sale of securities after $100 sales commission	4,400	(See page 30)

| | At Retirement | |
	Age 65	Age 62
2. Less federal, state, and local taxes on above	(500)	
Total additional after-tax income	$3,900	

In general, the Cash Expense Profile for age 62 reflects the same level of spending planned for normal retirement, adjusted for three fewer years of 5 percent inflation. Because the Williams' mortgage will not be paid up until Mike reaches 65, three additional years of payments will have to be made. Mike will also have to continue his annual life insurance premiums until age 65, and the Williamses will have to purchase some additional medical and dental insurance and replace the previous company-paid accident insurance policy. So, while cash expenses decrease, the reduction is small, from an estimate of $57,500 at 65 to $54,700 at 62. Now let's take a look at Mike and Doris's Cash Income Profile. The spread between cash income available (A) and cash income available after retirement (B) is much greater at age 62 than at 65, as follows:

	Age 65	Age 62
A. Total cash income at retirement	$61,600	$ 53,300
B. Cash income after retirement	53,600	40,200
"Spread"	($ 8,000)	($13,100)

The key reason for this is the reduction in Social Security income. Doris is not eligible to collect until age 62, and she's only 60 now. In addition, Mike's benefit at age 62 is reduced to 80 percent of his benefit at age 65. Further, his company pension plan also provides reduced benefits at age 62. As a result, if the Williamses change their retirement plans and use Mike's layoff by General Manufacturing as an opportunity to begin their retirement life-style earlier, they will have to add sources of income from their retirement net worth initially, and ultimately will have to change and limit their life-style. Retirement income will never reach the level it would have if Mike had retired at 65 and Doris at 63 as originally planned.

Look back at the Retirement Net Worth Profile on pages 18 and 19. There is $75,000 *less* in total resources available to finance their now-longer retirement. Also, if their spending remains the same, they will require $10,000 in *additional* retirement income to enjoy their present standard of living in their *first* year of retirement. (That's the difference in the additional after-tax income required to meet cash expenses at retirement at age 62, $14,500, and at age 65, $3,900.) And this amount will *increase* for the next two years, until Doris is eligible for modest Social Security benefits, and the mortgage and Mike's life insurance policy are paid up. We'll return to this scenario a little later.

Now it's time to review the projected retirement income status of Joan Stuart. Joan's Retirement Net Worth Profile is back on pages 21 and 22; her Cash Expense and Cash Income Profiles follow:

CASH EXPENSE PROFILE, JOAN STUART

	Today	At Retirement
A. Housing expenses		
1. Mortgage or rent	$6,000	$10,800
2. Real estate taxes—principal home	—	—
3. Real estate taxes—summer home	—	—
4. Utilities	1,400	2,500
5. Maintenance and repairs	—	—
6. Insurance	100	200
Total housing expenses	$7,500	$13,500

	Today	At Retirement
B. Food and personal expenses		
1. Dining at home	3,000	5,400
2. Dining out	700	1,300
3. Personal care	500	900
4. Clothing	800	1,400
5. Recreation	400	700
6. Furniture, appliances, etc.	500	900
7. All other:	500	900
Total food and personal expenses	$ 6,400	$11,500
C. Automobile expenses		
1. Loan payments, or savings to replace auto	1,800	3,200
2. Fuel, maintenance, and repairs	1,800	2,000
3. Insurance	500	1,100
Total automobile expenses	$ 3,500	$ 6,300
D. Travel expenses:	3,000	5,400
E. Life insurance—paid-up at age 65:	100	—
F. Supplemental medical insurance:	—	700
G. Gifts and contributions:	800	1,400
H. Savings	1,200	—
Total Cash Expenses	$22,500	$38,800

CASH INCOME PROFILE, JOAN STUART

	Today	At Retirement
A. From today to retirement		
1. Net income from salaries and wages, after all tax and other deductions	$22,900	$41,100
2. Interest received from savings accounts, certificates of deposit, etc.	1,400	2,500
3. Dividends received from investments in securities	—	—
4. Other income	—	—
5. Less estimated federal, state, and local taxes on items 2–4 above	(400)	(700)
Total cash income from today to retirement	$23,900	$42,900
B. Cash income after retirement		
1. Retirement income		
a. Social Security (½ taxable)		$16,900
b. Company pension plan (all taxable)		21,500
2. Interest and dividends from A2 and A3		2,500
3. Other income from A4, if applicable		—
4. Less federal, state, and local taxes on all of the above		(2,300)
Cash income before use of other assets		38,600
Less: cash expenses at retirement from Cash Expense Profile		38,800
Additional after-tax income required to meet cash expenses at retirement		$ 200

	Today	At Retirement
C. Sources of additonal after-tax income		
1. Savings		200
2. Less federal, state, and local taxes on above		—
Total additional after-tax income		$200

Joan Stuart's Cash Expense Profile reflects her relatively modest life-style. However, there is enough money for occasional vacation travel, dining out, and recreation. Joan has assumed that she will make no changes in her retirement, substituting local volunteer work and more reading for her present working hours. The Cash Income Profile on the preceding page indicates that despite only modest pension benefits, together with Social Security and interest on her savings, Joan is very close to her retirement income objective, needing only $200 in the first year of retirement to maintain her present standard of living.

But let's look more closely at Joan's situation. That $200 she needs comes from savings—the same savings that will generate $2,500 of interest income. That means the savings account balance shown in the Retirement Net Worth Profile on pages 21 and 22 will begin to *decline,* because Joan must use the interest *plus a part of the principal* to finance her retirement. To make matters worse, the company pension plan income is fixed at the same amount of $21,500 per year until Joan dies. Her expenses will continue to increase with inflation, and this will require additional withdrawals from her savings account. It is painfully obvious that she will run out of money well before she runs out of life expectancy—and what then? She almost certainly will have to abandon her dream of reading for pleasure and volunteer work.

Now is the time to take that leap into the pond of cold reality. We will move forward in time over the next twenty-five years to see how the Williamses and Joan Stuart fare under their preferred retirement scenarios:

LONG-RANGE RETIREMENT INCOME PLAN

	Year 0 At Retirement	Year 5	Year 10	Year 15	Year 20	Year 25
MIKE AND DORIS WILLIAMS						
Net retirement income	$53,600	$58,500	$66,700	$77,100	$90,500	$107,700
Expenses	57,500	73,400	93,900	119,800	152,900	195,000
Net income deficiency	3,900	14,900	27,200	42,700	62,400	87,300
Use of retirement net worth:						
Sale of securities	3,900	Asset exhausted in year 3 after retirement				
IRA—Mike		6,600	Asset exhausted in year 5			
IRA—Doris		8,300	Asset exhausted in year 6			
Employee investment fund—Mike			27,200	42,700	62,400	Asset exhausted in year 22
Sale of summer home and use of other assets						87,300
JOAN STUART						
Net retirement income	$40,100	$43,800	$45,900	$53,000	$61,900	$73,300
Expenses	38,800	49,400	63,100	80,600	102,800	131,100
Net income deficiency/(excess)	(1,300)	5,600	17,200	27,600	40,900	57,800
Use of retirement net worth:						
Savings account	(1,300)*	5,600	Asset exhausted in 10th year of retirement—all remaining assets must be sold to get through year 11 and expenses must be drastically reduced thereafter.			

* This modest excess of income over expenses occurs in the first year of retirement only and Ms. Stuart invested these funds in her savings account.

We have summarized the twenty-five-year retirement income plan to make it as understandable as possible. Since most of you *Pre-REtirement Planners* are not accountants or financial planners, the methods you should use to make your own calculations are covered in the next chapter. Some key assumptions have been made, which include holding to the 5 percent inflation rate for expenses and Social Security income and maintaining the same ratio of income taxes to gross income that we calculated for the Retirement Income Profiles at retirement. We also assumed that the interest earned by the Williamses and Joan Stuart on their employee investment, IRAs, and savings accounts would be added to those account balances *before* deducting any withdrawals or annual distributions.

The summary on the previous page shows that Mike and Doris Williams fell just short of adequately preparing for their retirement. Their assets were intended to be used for their retirement, and they used them well. Beginning with their first year of retirement, they sold their securities investments over a period of about three years. Then in year 4 they began to use Mike's IRA, and in year 5 Doris's IRA. In their sixth year of retirement, they began to draw on Mike's employee investment fund, which continued to increase from the deferred earnings and proved to be large enough to cover their retirement income needs until the twenty-second year. It was their intent from the outset to avoid selling either their principal residence or their summer home. However, if they hope to meet their twenty-five-year retirement objective of financial independence (Mike will then be 90 and Doris 88), they will have to sell their summer home in the twenty-second year after their retirement. Thus, to a minor degree they will not have achieved their overall objective.

As we have stated previously, we are working with many estimates and assumptions. You may recall that we assumed that Mike's employee investment fund would grow at 9 percent per year, well above the projected rate of inflation of 5 percent. If Mike's actual income growth is closer to the rate of inflation, he will fall short of his objective by several years.

But we are planning for the future now. Mike is 55, not 89, and he has just learned a valuable lesson from this exercise. If the Williamses remain healthy and live their full quota of years, and perhaps a few extra, they will fall just short of maintaining their retirement standard of living throughout the rest of their lives! Should Mike assume that he and

Doris will not live into extreme old age? Should he base his financial future on dying in his late 70s, with Doris to follow a few years later, in her early 80s? Given that scenario, his present financial plan will take care of their needs until the end. In fact, the family homestead, perhaps even the summer home, the family car, the $15,000 savings account, the balance of the employee investment fund, and the collection of ceramic figurines will all go to the kids as the *estate* of the late Mike and Doris Williams.

But can they bet against living into extreme old age? Certainly not! They have the time right now to make the modest corrections necessary to help assure their retirement income objective for an even longer period of time. For example:

1.   First, Mike can *immediately* raise his contribution to General Manufacturing's employee investment fund to the maximum permitted—that is, $4,000 per year, instead of the $3,000 he has been so inflexible about. With the company's contribution of $1,000, he will now be investing and earning interest on $5,000 today compared with $4,000. Mike predicted future growth of 9 percent per year during the Williams' retirement years. Obviously Mike will have to make some adjustments in how he now spends his money, such as reducing travel expenses, if he hopes to achieve this additional savings objective. By taking such action *now,* Mike and Doris will add substantially to their Retirement Net Worth Profile and future retirement income. The balance in the employee investment fund will increase from $203,000 at retirement to $218,000 at retirement, and provide for 1½ additional years of retirement income.

2.   Mike and Doris could also contribute $2,000 each, after taxes, to their IRA accounts. Interest earned by these deposits will continue to be tax-deferred until the funds are withdrawn. As with the additional contribution to the employee fund, there is one problem with this strategy: Where will the money come from? Doris enjoys her job at the local mall, but it is nothing special and has no potential. She has thought often of working elsewhere where her sales ability would be more properly rewarded. As Mike and Doris explore alternatives for saving more while not giving up any of their well-deserved present luxuries, Doris may suggest that perhaps she should look for a new job. With a

little effort, she may find a sales position that could increase her earnings.

3. Mike and Doris may also consider an adjustment in housing plans. While this decision doesn't have to be made now, the Williamses should begin to think about how they can reduce the cost of owning a principal home and a vacation home. By selling one or both and replacing them with smaller, easier-to-manage homes, the Williamses can add cash for investment and reduce housing expenses because of lower maintenance, taxes, and related costs. The present houses were designed for a larger family. Now that there are only two in the family, a more modest house may be desirable.

4. While it is always difficult to change, the Williamses (and any *Pre-REtirement Planners*) should think through changes that will not significantly affect their life-style. Look for alternative ways to achieve substantially the same life-style but also increase your retirement net worth or your retirement income, or reduce your retirement expense levels.

Let's return to the early-retirement scenario for a moment. One reality for the Williamses has now become quite clear: they cannot afford to take early retirement, nor have they done their financial planning with early retirement in mind. They do not have, nor can they build at this late date, the resources for early retirement. As it stands now, with normal retirement, they must make some modest adjustments to assure maintenance of their pre-retirement standard of living for *all* of their retirement years.

Sometimes, no matter how well we plan, we're forced into early retirement and have to deal with it. But we shouldn't deal with it passively, not without making the most energetic effort to restore lost income and the lost opportunity for additional retirement income. For example, Doris certainly is not ready for retirement. By now she has probably landed that better sales job and, as originally planned, wants to stay on until she's 63. Nor is Mike ready to retire. He's in good health and full of the old vigor. He's ready for new challenges and opportunities. One should not minimize the difficulties Mike will have finding a new position at 62, but there are many, many careers that were started anew at more advanced ages than that. Although he'll have a hard time finding a corporate job on his previous level, there are smaller organizations that can use his experience and solid work ethic. He doubtless won't be paid as handsomely as in the past, and he'll lose some retirement income possibilities. That simply means he'll have to save even more and perhaps be extra-careful with his investments to assure the most acceptable yield, while maintaining the safety of his investments so they'll be available for retirement.

The Williamses will make appropriate changes and move forward. They know what their retirement objectives are, and they will continue to focus on them, adjusting for changing conditions as they go along.

Joan Stuart's financial planning, in contrast, suggests a rather serious shortfall in retirement income. She will run out of savings in the tenth year of her retirement, at age 75. Again, Joan is a *Pre-REtirement Planner*; she is currently 53 years old, and she is not planning to make herself destitute at age 75. On the contrary, she is planning to maintain her pre-retirement standard of living for the rest of her life. Joan is already saving a reasonable proportion of her after-tax earnings at 5 percent. Her major problem is her modest income. She has a decent pension plan, which many smaller companies do not offer. Joan should consider the following ideas to help solve her financial problems:

1. She could transfer most of the present passbook savings and certificates of deposit into longer-term, higher-yielding investments such as government-backed zero coupon bonds. (See chapter 5 for descriptions of these investments.) She should keep only a modest savings balance for emergencies.

2. She could find a higher-paying job with an organization that has at least as good a pension plan, after thoroughly understanding the effect that leaving her present employer will have on her total pension income, and then put *all* of the additional after-tax income into relatively safe, growth-type investments with higher yields than the present savings accounts.

3. She could take a part-time job for two or three evenings a week or on weekends and use the income as suggested above.

4. She could purchase a two-family house, using part of the current savings as a down payment. If net costs after taxes can be kept

the same as present rent expenses, Joan will be able to help offset future inflation. While fixed-rate mortgage payments remain the same over the life of the mortgage, the income from the apartment will *grow* with inflation. Joan will also have a valuable asset which could be sold to provide retirement income by the time she reaches her mid-70s.

5. She could purchase a small condominium or cooperative apartment, using part of present savings as a down payment. This may also help fix monthly housing costs and provide an asset for future retirement income.

One further point before we leave this chapter. It is quite possible that your pre-retirement spending levels are so high that it is impossible for you to achieve the same spending level in retirement. The case studies we have reviewed and the procedures that will be summarized in the next chapter are designed to get you to take a hard look at what you are doing now and where you are going in the future. In many cases, it is necessary to reduce spending down to the levels of retirement income. That does suggest that we will not achieve our original objective: *to maintain your pre-retirement standard of living for the rest of your life.* Some of you will be stuck with inadequate—or possibly no—company pension plans. You will have to rely on Social Security and your own savings, IRA, securities investments, etc. for retirement income. It is probably impossible for you to achieve your pre-retirement standard of living without a windfall such as an inheritance. Therefore, you will have to reduce spending or increase income through part-time work, or remain fully employed beyond the age you originally thought you would want to retire. There are trade-offs, and you are the one who has to decide which is more important: current consumption and leisure—or *financial independence later!*

4

Your Retirement Net Worth, Expense, and Income Profiles

Now that you're familiar with our case studies, you are ready to prepare your own retirement financial plan, one that will serve your double-edged objective: *to assure financial independence and to maintain your pre-retirement standard of living for the rest of your life.* All of your financial planning must focus on these twin objectives.

We hope you will start your financial planning process now! Some of you may find it more convenient to start your plan after the preparation of your annual federal and, if appropriate, state and local income tax returns. Much of the same information you may gather to prepare your tax returns, or to provide information and evidence to a professional tax-return preparer, is required for your retirement financial plan.

Refer to the worksheets in the Appendix for the information you should collect for your planning effort. Do all your gathering at the beginning. When you're in the middle of the process, you don't want to be interrupted having to search for papers and figures.

Once you have all the information you need to prepare your plan, you're going to proceed in the same order we did when we reviewed the planning for the Williamses and Joan Stuart. First, you'll prepare a Retirement Net Worth Profile, then a Cash Expense Profile, and then a Cash Income Profile, which also compares cash expenses to cash income at retirement and shows the amount, if any, of additional after-tax income required to meet cash expenses once you retire. You will then identify the initial sources from your Net Worth Profile that will be used to cover any deficiency in retirement income. As you remember, the total of your Cash Expense Profile is your initial retirement income objective. You will then need to complete one additional form: your Long-Range Retirement Income Plan, which we summarized on page 42 for our two case studies. This is a critical part of your planning effort, because it helps you to determine whether or not you are saving sufficiently today to protect your retirement income for the long-term future. We have assumed that the retirement period will total twenty-five years from normal retirement at age 65.

Let's begin with the Retirement Net Worth Profile. The form is the same as the models we reviewed earlier. However, you should feel free to add items that may not be covered, or to utilize your own format. We have provided a set of worksheets at the back of the book for your convenience, which you can either cut out or duplicate.

RETIREMENT NET WORTH PROFILE

Assets	Today	At Retirement
1. Cash on hand and in bank accounts, certificates of deposit, etc., which you can gain access to immediately, even if there is a penalty		
2. Securities, including bonds, common and preferred stocks, government securities, mutual funds, etc.		
3. Cash value of company employee investment fund or other company savings plans, etc.		
4. Cash value of IRA accounts and Keoghs (HR 10) Husband: Wife:		

Assets	Today	At Retirement
5. Cash surrender values of life insurance policies		
6. Value of your home		
7. Value of any other real estate investments, summer houses, etc.		
8. Value of your full- or part-time business		
9. Value of your cars		
10. Value of any collectibles, gold, jewelry, furs, etc.		

TOTAL ASSETS

LIABILITIES

1. Remaining principal due on mortgages on your home and any real estate investments		
2. Balance of car loan		
3. Balance of any bank loans, personal debt, credit cards, charge accounts, etc.		

TOTAL LIABILITIES
RETIREMENT NET WORTH

We will now give you some guides to help you complete this important information. As was previously illustrated, you must make some assumptions in order to get from "Today" to "At Retirement." These include the rate of inflation, interest rates and returns for various types of investments, dividend rates, and the rate of appreciation in the value of real estate. Each asset you list under "Today" requires an assumption of growth to estimate your "At Retirement" balance. List each of these assumptions next to the asset identified on the form or on a separate worksheet. When you reexamine your estimates a year from now, you should know what assumptions you made at this time. Should those assumptions prove incorrect, you will then know what changes to make.

The following takes you through several calculations which you can use as a model for your own efforts. In this case, the planned retirement date is *seven years in the future.*

ASSETS, line 1. Let's assume you have a single savings account at City Savings Bank, with a balance today of $8,000; the interest rate is 5 percent per annum.

Assumption: Interest rate will remain at 5 percent per year.

At retirement: The balance will have grown at an annual rate of 5 percent for a period of seven years. Look at Table 1, The Future Value of $1, on page 00 and go down the period column to 7, then look across to the column under 5 percent for the factor: 1.407. Multiply the $8,000 balance by 1.407. The result is $11,256.

Let's also assume you are making annual deposits of $500 to this account. The value of this annual deposit, which will also earn interest at 5 percent per year, can be determined by consulting Table 2, The Future Value of an Annuity of One Dollar for *N* Periods on page 14. Find 7 (for seven years) under the ''Period'' column and look across to the 5 percent column. The factor is 8.142 and the result is $4,071 ($500 × 8.142 = $4,071). That is the result of depositing $500 per year for seven years at a yearly interest of 5 percent in your savings account.

Now, adding the $11,256 calculated previously for the current savings account balance at retirement to the $4,071 resulting from annual additions to savings from now to retirement, we have a total of $15,327. Round this amount to either $15,000 or $15,300, as you prefer, and enter it on line 1 under the heading ''At Retirement.''

ASSETS, line 2. You own 200 shares of a major oil company common stock which has paid a dividend of $1 per share for the past two years. The stock is currently selling for $25 per share on the New York Stock Exchange. The total value today is $5,000, and the dividend yield is 4 percent per year (the $1 annual dividend divided by $25). You believe this solid stock will do no worse than parallel inflation over the next seven years until your retirement. You have not been reinvesting the dividends; you have used them for spending and/or savings in other areas.

Assumption: The value of the stock will increase at the estimated rate of inflation of 5 percent per year. The annual dividend will be spent or invested in other areas. Make the same calculation as was made for the current savings account balance, using the factor of 1.407 from page 11. The result is $7,035 ($5,000 × 1.407 = $7,035), which is rounded to $7,000. Enter this amount on line 2 under the heading ''At Retirement.''

You should use the procedures discussed in the foregoing examples for all your investments, starting with their present market or cash value, adding your reasonable estimate for increased market value and for growth from reinvesting interest and dividends, and also adding any new investments you plan to make. However, if you spend the interest or dividends, do not include such funds as an asset.

If you read carefully through the case studies, follow the foregoing examples and suggestions, collect the information suggested in the worksheets in the Appendix, and review and give some thought to the various assets and liabilities shown on the Retirement Net Worth Profile, you should successfully complete this part of your retirement planning effort.

Your Cash Expense Profile form follows. Refer to Chapter 3 for discussion of the case studies. Pay particular attention to those expenses that will change at your planned retirement date. For example, many of us will have satisfied our mortgage debts by retirement; this important expense will therefore be eliminated at retirement. Also be sure to provide for increases in expenses resulting from inflation. If you assume, as you did with interest rates, that expenses will increase at an annual rate of 5 percent, then use the table on page 11. It will give you the factor to apply to today's expenses in order to determine the ''At Retirement'' expense.

CASH EXPENSE PROFILE

	Today	At Retirement
A. Housing expenses		
1. Mortgage		
2. Real estate taxes—principal home		
3. Real estate taxes—summer home		
4. Utilities		
5. Maintenance and repairs		
6. Insurance		
Total housing expenses		
B. Food and personal expenses		
1. Dining at home		
2. Dining out		
3. Personal care		
4. Clothing		
5. Recreation		
6. Furniture, appliances, etc.		
7. All other		
Total food and personal expenses		
C. Automobile expenses		
1. Loan payments, or savings to replace auto		
2. Fuel, maintenance, and repairs		
3. Insurance		
Total automobile expenses		

	Today	At Retirement
D. Travel expenses		
E. Life insurance—paid-up at age 65		
F. Medical, dental, and accident insurance		
G. Gifts and contributions		
H. Savings		

TOTAL CASH EXPENSES

Also, carefully review your retirement medical and dental insurance options. Does your company provide you with free medical insurance at retirement? If not, you should allow for the cost of medical and dental insurance, and the annual deductibles you're required to pay. This should be entered on line F.

SAVINGS

Unlike the previous cash expense profiles, this one includes a new bottom line, savings, which of course is the extent to which your income exceeds expenses. You should include in the "Today" column any monies you are presently investing in your savings accounts, government bonds, stocks, and other securities. These are the funds you are saving toward retirement. At retirement you will probably eliminate most or all of these savings and investments. Do *not* include any *payroll deductions* for company investment or savings plans, or U.S. Savings Bonds. Later, when you prepare your Cash Income Profile, you will start with your net cash income from salaries and wages *after* such deductions.

Use care in completing this profile and be sure to identify *all* of your current spending. When completed, your Cash Expense Profile will represent your Initial Retirement Income Objective—the level of spending you believe will allow you to continue your present standard of living after retirement.

The next form, the Cash Income Profile, provides you with the information you need to determine whether or not you can achieve enough income at retirement to cover your total cash expenses. If you find yourself in trouble, you must determine which assets from your Retirement Net Worth Profile should be used to cover any deficiency in retirement income.

CASH INCOME PROFILE

	Today	At Retirement
A. From today to retirement		
1. Net income from salaries and wages after all tax and other deductions		
2. Interest received from savings accounts, certificates of deposit, etc.		
3. Dividends received from investments in securities		
4. Other income		
5. Less estimated federal, state, and local taxes on items 2–4 above		
Total cash income from today to retirement		
B. Cash income after retirement		
1. Retirement income		
a. Social Security (partly taxable)		
b. Company pension plan (all taxable)		
2. Interest and dividends from A2 and A3		

	Today	At Retirement
3. Other income from A4, if applicable		
4. Less federal, state, and local taxes on all of the above		
Cash income before use of other assets		
Less: cash expenses at retirement from Cash Expense Profile		
Additional after-tax income required to meet cash expenses at retirement		

C. Sources of additional after-tax income

1. Withdrawals from savings accounts, proceeds from certificates of deposit, and sale of securities (partly taxable)

2. Withdrawals from IRAs, company employee fund, or other savings plans (partly taxable)

3. Less federal, state, and local taxes on above

Total additional after-tax income required

The following information will help you complete your Cash Income Profile:

INCOME PROFILE:

SECTION A, FOR THE "TODAY" COLUMN

Line 1: Indicate your present net take-home income from your employment and that of your spouse for the current year. This can be determined by multiplying your net take-home pay by the number of pay periods in the year. In making this calculation, include only the net amount actually payable to you in your periodic paycheck. The deductions for company savings plans and savings bonds have already been accounted for in the Retirement Net Worth Profile and you must therefore indicate your net income *after* such deductions here.

Line 2: Include all interest income actually received or credited to your savings accounts. If you reinvest this interest income, it should also be included in your Cash Expense Profile on the last line.

Line 3: Dividends should be treated the same as interest.

Line 4: Other income includes all other forms of income. If you have several different types of such income, prepare separate estimates of each and show the total on this line. For example, you might own an interest in a business that provides cash distributions to you.

Line 5: All income taxes on interest, dividends, and other income should be included on this line. You have already provided for income taxes applicable to your salary and wages by showing your net take-home cash income on line 1.

The amounts to be indicated in the "At Retirement" column should also be estimated based on your reasonable expectations from today until your retirement. Again, indicate what your assumptions are and use the tables we explained earlier to calculate your "At Retirement" estimates. You will also find the case studies helpful in thinking through these estimates.

SECTION B

Line 1a: Social Security income can be estimated based on the procedure described in chapter 6. Note that Social Security income may be taxable up to a maximum of one-half (50 percent) of such income.

Line 1b: Your pension income at your planned retirement date can be estimated from your company pension plan's descriptive material or by calling your company personnel department and requesting such information. You should understand your company pension plan options and include an estimate that reflects the option most appropriate for you.

Line 2: Interest and dividend income should be the same under "At Retirement" as indicated on lines A2 and A3.

Line 3: Other income should be reflected in accordance with your plans.

Line 4: Federal, state, and local taxes on all of the above will require some computation. Since no one knows what will happen to income tax rates beyond this—and perhaps next—year, it may be appropriate for you to assume that the percentage of income taxes to adjusted gross income as of "Today" be retained for "At Retirement." That means if your total federal, state, and local income taxes are now 25 percent of your adjusted gross income, assume they will average the same 25 percent at retirement.

The total of section B is your cash income after retirement, applicable to the first year of retirement only. Next, transfer your cash expenses at retirement from your Cash Expense Profile. Subtract this amount from the total cash income. The remainder is the additional after-tax income required to meet cash expenses at retirement. You will be faced with a retirement income GAP if your cash expenses are higher than your cash income. For example:

Cash income before sale of assets	$40,000
Less cash expense at retirement from Cash Expense Profile	45,000
Additional after-tax income required to meet cash expenses at retirement (GAP)	$5,000

It is also possible that your Cash Expense Profile will show total expenses of, say, $38,000. Then there is no GAP but instead a *surplus* of $2,000 for the first year of retirement, which can be invested for future retirement needs. But the chances are you will have a GAP between retirement income and expenses that will need to be filled by using the assets included in your Retirement Net Worth Profile.

In the unlikely event you do have an initial surplus, do not complete Section C of the form. Instead, go back to your Cash Expense Profile and add to the bottom line the amount of surplus that will now be invested. Also, return to your Retirement Net Worth Profile (pages 49 and 50) and add the same amount to your savings or other investments as is appropriate, in the "At Retirement" column.

If you are the typical *Pre-REtirement Planner*, your next step is to identify the sources to cover your GAP. Here are some logical steps to follow in choosing the correct assets to be converted into cash:

1. When you retire, it is to your advantage first to use those assets that produce fully taxable income. For example, if you have *more* than an appropriate emergency fund (such as six months of income) in cash, CDs, or short-term government instruments, begin to draw on those balances. Generally, such investments pay the lowest rates of interest and the income is fully taxable. Remember, *the first place you look for additional retirement funds is in fully taxed assets.*

2. Next, sell stocks, bonds, and other similar investments that produce fully taxable dividends or interest income. You will have to pay taxes on any capital gains realized from the sale of such securities.

3. Sell other assets, such as real estate holdings. However, if you are considering the sale of rental real estate, be sure you fully understand the effect on your retirement of lost rental income as well as the loss of any depreciation tax benefits.

4. If you are not yet 70½, you will not be required to withdraw from your IRA, Keogh, or 401(k) plans. *And don't. You should postpone withdrawals from these investments as long as legally possible, because all income is 100 percent tax-deferred.* However, once you reach 70½ you must start to make withdrawals. Once you are forced to withdraw from these plans, you must pay full income taxes on the portion of such withdrawal that represents your before-tax contributions and deferred interest income, as well as appreciation of any common stocks or other investments that may be included in the plan balance. Withdrawals that represent after-tax contributions you may have made to the plan will be tax-free. Further, you will continue to enjoy tax deferral of the income earned by these plans as long as there is a balance remaining.

5. If you own your own home, you may have to sell it to help finance your retirement. Alternatively, you may find it advantageous to raise retirement funds through a home equity loan or a new mortgage on your home. Before you make any decisions on loans that use your home as collateral, be sure to investigate all of the available types of private and public financing opportunities being offered to retirees in your state. The mortgage officer at your local bank and your local senior citizens' assistance agencies and organizations are good places to start.

Our final form is the Long-Range Retirement Income Plan. Each of the profiles we have just reviewed is important in determining your retirement income objective and in planning how that objective will be achieved. It was necessary for us to show you how to plan from today to retirement in order to estimate your financial condition for your first retirement year. You now know what your Retirement Net Worth is; you have determined your Initial Retirement Income Objective, your GAP, if any, and the resources you will use from your Retirement Net Profile to cover that GAP.

But remember—this is only for your *first year of retirement*. Now we will deal with the toughest part of our planning effort: projecting your retirement expenses and income over the rest of your life. That's what the Williamses and Joan Stuart did (as summarized on page 42), and that's what you must do so that you don't come up short and sorry way down the line. As stated earlier, you should use at least twenty-five years for this planning process, from age 65 to age 90. If you have a spouse and she or he is close to your age, you may wish to use your age as the basis for your planning. If the spouse is younger, use a longer time period, but we suggest you use the target age of 90 for both spouses. For example, if your planned retirement age is 65, and your spouse will be 62 at that time, you will need to plan twenty-eight years of retirement to reach age 90.

The form on the following page reflects a planning horizon of twenty-five years.

Here are some suggestions for completing the required information and projecting over the twenty-five year period. You should generally fill in the "Year 0 at Retirement" column from the information you already have in your Cash Expense Profile and Cash Income Profile. Simply transfer the numbers to this form. In the case of cash expenses, start with the total of the Cash Expense Profile and proceed as follows:

SECTION A

You should assume that your cash expenses will continue for the twenty-five-year planning period and will increase at the average annual inflation rate of 5 percent. We have reviewed the procedure for making these projections previously, but let's go through them once again. Refer

LONG-RANGE RETIREMENT INCOME PLAN

	Year 0 at Retirement	Year 5	Year 10	Year 15	Year 20	Year 25
A. Cash expenses						
1. _____	_____	_____	_____	_____	_____	_____
2. _____	_____	_____	_____	_____	_____	_____
3. _____	_____	_____	_____	_____	_____	_____
4. _____	_____	_____	_____	_____	_____	_____
5. _____	_____	_____	_____	_____	_____	_____
Total cash expenses	_____	_____	_____	_____	_____	_____
B. Cash income						
1. Social security	_____	_____	_____	_____	_____	_____
2. Company pension	_____	_____	_____	_____	_____	_____
3. Interest/dividends	_____	_____	_____	_____	_____	_____
4. Other income	_____	_____	_____	_____	_____	_____
5. _____	_____	_____	_____	_____	_____	_____
6. Less-income taxes	_____	_____	_____	_____	_____	_____
Net cash income	_____	_____	_____	_____	_____	_____
GAP/(surplus) before additional income	_____	_____	_____	_____	_____	_____
C. Sources of additional income						
1. Excess savings	_____	_____	_____	_____	_____	_____
2. Sale of securities	_____	_____	_____	_____	_____	_____
3. Sale of other investments	_____	_____	_____	_____	_____	_____
4. 401(k) plan	_____	_____	_____	_____	_____	_____
5. IRA, Keogh plans	_____	_____	_____	_____	_____	_____
6. _____	_____	_____	_____	_____	_____	_____
7. _____	_____	_____	_____	_____	_____	_____
8. Less-income taxes	_____	_____	_____	_____	_____	_____
Total additional income	_____	_____	_____	_____	_____	_____
Total all income	_____	_____	_____	_____	_____	_____
GAP/(surplus)	_____	_____	_____	_____	_____	_____

to Table 1, The Future Value of One Dollar. To calculate the inflated value of your "At Retirement" cash expenses in year 5, go to number 5 under the "Period" column. Reading across to the right, under the 5 percent column you will see the factor 1.276. Multiply the amount you previously entered on the form for year 0 cash expenses by this factor. Enter the result, rounded to the nearest thousand or hundred, in the year 5 column. Each of the subsequent planning periods are also spaced five years apart. The same factor is applicable to these periods. Multiply by this factor the amount you entered for cash expenses under the "Year 5" column and place the result, after rounding, under the "Year 10" heading. Then repeat this process for each five-year period. This will tell you what your planned cash expenditures at retirement will increase to by year 5 and in five-year increments thereafter. Using our earlier example, $40,000 in cash expenditures in the first year of retirement will grow to $51,000 by the end of year 5, $65,000 by year 10, and a whopping $135,000 by year 25—or more than three times the original "At Retirement" estimate!

We have made two key assumptions. First, you will not change any spending patterns during retirement, and second, inflation will average 5 percent per year. There are blank spaces on the form to enable you to be more precise with your assumptions, if there's a good chance you'll be making changes as you grow older. For example, you may be an avid sailing enthusiast and spend large sums to own and maintain a 36-foot sailboat. You may decide that it would make better financial sense to give up that hobby at year 10 of your retirement.

SECTION B

In this section, every element of income identified in your Cash Income Profile must be repeated. The reality of fixed income and the necessity of converting assets to cash will become apparent. Begin this section by entering the amounts in the "Year 0" column from your Cash Income Profile.

LINE 1: Social Security should grow at the rate of inflation, using the same factors and method discussed above for section A. It is important, however, that you stay abreast of Social Security rule changes. There is a current provision in the law which can eliminate cost-of-living increases.

LINE 2: Pensions generally do not increase with inflation. Most are fixed for life. If your pension is $20,000 in your first year of retirement, it will be $20,000 in year 25 as well. As we just noted, inflation will increase expenses by more than three times in twenty-five years. The buying power of this fixed pension income will, therefore, decline to less than one-third over the twenty-five-year period.

LINE 3: In general, if the amount of the investment is fixed, such as a savings account, the interest income will be about the same each year. Naturally, if you reinvest the interest in additional savings, the total balance in the savings account will increase and the interest will increase proportionately. Dividends on common stock should tend to increase. Your estimates may be based on past growth or expectations of the firm's future performance.

LINE 4: Other income should be estimated consistent with your experience and reasonable expectations of future growth. Err on the conservative side.

LINE 5: Income taxes represent a significant assumption that needs to be reviewed each year. As we indicated earlier, we assumed that the federal, state, and local tax rates as a percent of adjusted gross income in effect in 1988 would continue throughout our planning. If in 1988 this rate for you was 25 percent, use the same rate for each year of your long-range retirement plan, with one exception. Only 50 percent of Social Security income may be taxable. If your Social Security is taxable, use only 50 percent of the line 1 totals when you apply your effective income tax rate to lines 1 through 5. That will result in an amount for income taxes for each period that is lower than your present rate.

Your net cash income should be subtracted from your total cash expenses to determine your GAP (income less than expenses) or surplus (income more than expenses). While you may have a surplus in year 1, by year 5 or 10 you will almost certainly have a GAP. It is this amount which must be covered from the assets in your Net Worth Profile. Most of these assets were acquired ''for the future,'' and that future has now arrived.

SECTION C

Here is where you must determine the priority order of assets to be converted to retirement income. This is your decision but should reflect our earlier discussion, which suggested that you maintain tax-deferred accounts (for example, IRAs) as long as possible.

As you complete your planning, you will realize that most, perhaps all, of your assets at retirement will be required to finance your retirement. If assets remain, such as your home, and perhaps some investments, these will be your estate and will be distributed according to your will. While this book does not focus on estate planning, you should have a valid will whether or not you expect to leave many assets behind. If your estate is substantial, you should also seek the professional tax advice necessary to reduce estate taxes which will be paid out of your estate by your executor.

It is a hard truth that your GAP at retirement will grow over the years as inflation drives expenses above your partially fixed income. If your Net Worth Profile is large enough, you may be able to cover that increasing GAP. In that case you're very fortunate indeed and definitely in the minority of *Pre-REtirement Planners*.

Most of us will find this first planning effort to be something of a rude awakening to the realities of retirement economics. We will have learned some fundamental facts of life that should be applied immediately:

1. Current income should be maximized. Changing jobs or taking on part-time work may increase funds to invest for retirement. If you're in a job without a pension plan, investigate changing jobs to a company that provides one!

2. Current spending should be scrutinized and changes made to provide additional funds to invest for retirement.

3. Current investment programs and habits should be rethought to assure maximum returns consistent with the need to protect principal for retirement.

4. Contributions to tax-deferred retirements plans (401(k), IRA, and Keogh plans) should be increased as provided by employers and in accordance with current tax law.

5.   Your retirement plans and expectations should be reviewed once each year.

6.   You should make a modest investment in your future by consulting a qualified professional on your unique retirement financial planning needs. Use the material in the next chapter to help you understand the large variety of investments available.

5

Looking at Investment Alternatives

You are reading this book because you are interested in learning more about how to prepare for eventual retirement. You might be a person in your mid-30s looking for information that will help you make the right decisions to build assets for your retirement thirty years from now. Or you may be 64, preparing to retire within months or in a year or two. At age 64 and age 35, *Pre-REtirement Planners* will select somewhat different investment objectives. These are decisions that ultimately you must make for yourself—decisions that reflect your willingness and ability to bear risk, as well as your age. We cannot make these decisions for you, but we can point you toward possible solutions.

First, let's look at a small but important segment of investment history:

In 1972, Xerox common stock reached an all-time high of 171⅞ per share. Fifteen years later Xerox's common stock was trading at 60, which was 65 percent below its historic high. In 1970, Federal Express did not exist, but if an investor had bought Federal Express shares when they were initially sold for $3 to the general public on April 12, 1978,

Some of the material in this chapter is derived from Herbert B. Mayo, *Investments: An Introduction,* Hinsdale, Illinois: The Dryden Press, 1988. Permission to use this material has been graciously given by the publisher. All rights reserved.

that investor would have watched the shares appreciate over 1,800 percent within eight years. It was not until 1975 that Americans could legally own gold bullion. At that time gold traded for about $200 an ounce; its price rose to more than $800 an ounce during 1980. Prior to 1975, individuals deposited funds in savings accounts at commercial banks because one of today's most popular investments, shares in money market mutual funds, was not available.

What a dynamic history investments have had! And what meaning investments can have for you *Pre-REtirement Planners*! Over the years some investments have produced extraordinary gains, while others have produced only mediocre returns, and still others substantial losses. Today the field of investment is even more dynamic than it was only a decade ago because there are so many to choose among. Events occur so rapidly—events that can and do alter the value of specific assets. The amount of information available to the investor is staggering and continually growing. The development of home computers will increase our ability to track investments and perform investment analysis. Furthermore, the inflation of the 1970s and early 1980s has made us all more aware of the importance of financial planning and wise investing.

YOUR PORTFOLIO

Whenever you receive income, there are two choices: you can either save your money or spend it. If you decide to save, an additional decision must be made: What's to be done with the savings? This is an extremely important question because in 1986, Americans' personal income was $3,534.3 billion and they saved 130.6 billion. The saver must decide where to invest this command over goods and services that's currently not being used. This is a crucial decision, particularly for the *Pre-REtirement Planner*, because these assets are the means by which today's purchasing power is transferred to the future. In effect, the saver must decide on a *portfolio* of assets to own. A portfolio is a combination of assets designed to serve as a store of value. Poor management of these assets may destroy the portfolio's value as well as the investor's chance to achieve his or her investment goals in retirement.

And a *Pre-REtirement Planner*'s goal, which cannot be stated often enough, is to *achieve financial independence for the rest of his or her life*. Investing will often play a key role in reaching this goal.

There are many motives for saving and accumulating assets, and planning for retirement is one of the chief among them. Your motive for saving affects the composition of the portfolio. Savings that are held to meet emergencies should not be invested in assets whose potential return involves substantial risk; instead, emphasis should be placed on assets with an assured return that can be readily converted to cash, such as savings accounts. A portfolio that is designed to help finance retirement can stress long-term assets, such as bonds that will mature many years in the future or stocks that offer potential growth in value.

The *Pre-REtirement Planner*'s capacity or willingness to bear risk plays an important role in constructing the portfolio. Some individuals are more willing and able to bear risk than others, and they will tend to select assets on which the return involves greater risk to obtain the specified investment goals. For example, if the saver wants to build a retirement fund, he or she can choose from a variety of possible investments. However, not all investments are equal in terms of risk and potential return. Those investors who are more willing to accept risk may construct portfolios with assets involving greater risk that may earn higher returns. Although conservative investors may select securities issued by the more financially stable firms, investors who are less averse to taking risk may select stocks issued by younger, less seasoned firms that may offer better opportunities for growth over a period of years. Mike and Doris Williams, as we have seen, have tended toward conservative employment of their assets. On the other hand, there are *Pre-REtirement Planners* with a great deal of discretionary income who may choose the avenue of greater risks for greater rewards.

Taxes also help to decide the composition of your portfolio. Investments are subject to a variety of different taxes. The income that is generated is taxed, as is the capital appreciation that is realized. Some states levy personal property taxes on securities. When a person dies, the federal government taxes the value of the estate, which includes the portfolio. In addition to the federal estate tax, several states tax the distribution of the wealth (that is, they levy a tax on an individual's inheritance). Such taxes and the desire to reduce them affect the composition of each person's portfolio.

INVESTMENT GOALS

The purpose of investing is to transfer purchasing power from the present to the future. A portfolio is a store of value designed to meet the individual investors's rationale—in this case, retirement—for postponing the consumption of goods and services from the present to the future.

The *Pre-REtirement Planner* has a wide variety of assets to choose from for investment, and within each type of asset there is an almost unlimited number of choices. However, every asset can be compared with other assets in terms of certain common characteristics: liquidity, marketability, potential income and/or capital gains, risk, and tax implications. The summary on page 70 lists the major classes of assets and summarizes their characteristics.

The first two characteristics listed are the asset's liquidity and marketability. Liquidity is the ease of converting the asset into cash with little risk of loss. NOW accounts, savings accounts, shares in money market mutual funds, and Treasury bills are very liquid assets, since there is virtually no chance of loss of principal. However, only Treasury bills are also marketable. There is no secondary market for NOW and savings accounts because the saver simply withdraws the funds on demand, and shares in money market mutual funds are redeemed—that is, sold back to the fund.

Many assets that are marketable are not truly liquid, as there is the potential for loss. Without the existence of secondary markets there would be no way for the investor to convert the asset back to cash. These markets may be very well developed and organized, as in the case of stock traded on the New York Stock Exchange, or poorly developed and very informal, as in the secondary market for collectibles.

Every asset offers a potential return that comes either through income, such as interest or dividends, or through capital gains. Capital gains offer a modest tax advantage, since the tax is deferred until the gain is realized. The possibility of such returns for each type of asset is indicated. The next column presents the federal income tax status of each type of asset. The returns earned by most assets are taxable at the federal level, but there are major exceptions, such as the interest earned on municipal bonds. Other assets, such as real estate, permit the deferral of tax, as the funds generated by the investment are sheltered from income taxes by expenses such as noncash depreciation charges.

A SUMMARY OF INVESTMENT ALTERNATIVES AND THEIR CHARACTERISTICS

Asset	Liquidity	Marketability	Return: Possible Income	Possible Capital Gains	Tax Status	Sources of Risk
Money	Complete	None	No	No	None	Purchasing power risk
NOW and savings accounts	High	None	Yes	No	Taxable	Meager purchasing power risk (risk-free up to $100,000)[1]
Certificates of deposit	High	None	Yes	No	Taxable	Meager purchasing power risk (risk-free up to $100,000)
Money market mutual funds	High	None	Yes	No	Taxable	Meager purchasing power risk (virtually risk-free)[1]
Quality corporate bonds	Moderate	Yes	Yes	Yes[2]	Taxable	Business/financial/interest rate/purchasing power risk
Lower-rated corporate bonds	Moderate to little	Moderate	Yes	Yes[2]	Taxable	Business/financial/interest rate/purchasing power risk
Preferred stock	Moderate	Moderate	Yes	Yes	Taxable	Business/financial/interest rate/purchasing power risk
Treasury bills	High	Yes	Yes	No	Taxable[3]	Meager purchasing power risk (virtually risk-free)[1]
Treasury bonds	Moderate	Yes	Yes	Yes	Taxable[3]	Purchasing power/ interest rate risk
Municipal bonds	Moderate to little	Yes	Yes	Yes[2]	Nontaxable[4]	Purchasing power/ interest rate risk
EE and HH bonds	High	None	Yes	No	Taxable[3]	Purchasing power risk[1]
Federal agency bonds	Moderate	Yes	Yes	Yes[2]	Taxable[3]	Purchasing power/ interest rate risk
Quality common stock	Moderate	Yes	Yes	Yes	Taxable	Business/financial/ market/purchasing power risk
Speculative common stock	Little	Moderate	In selective cases	Yes	Taxable	Business/financial/ market/purchasing power risk
Mutual funds	Moderate	None (shares redeemed)	Yes	Yes	Taxable[5]	Market/purchasing power risk

[1] Yields may adjust to offset purchasing power risk.

[2] Capital gains do not apply to zero coupon bonds, bonds sold initially at a discount, or bonds issued after July 18, 1984, and bought at a discount.

[3] Interest is not taxable at the state and local level.

[4] Interest on nontaxable bonds may be taxable at the state and local level.

[5] Mutual funds that invest in state and local government securities are tax-exempt.

The last column reviews the sources of risk. Since the future is uncertain, the investor must bear risk to earn a return. There is the risk applicable only to the specific asset, and for firms it covers the nature of the operation (business risk) and how the firm is financed (financial risk). This risk can be reduced through the construction of diversified portfolios, but other sources of risk are still important. These sources of risk include market risk, interest rate risk, and loss of purchasing power. Those assets whose returns tend to fluctuate with fluctuations in the market as a whole have market risk. Assets whose prices are sensitive to changes in interest rates have interest rate risk.

Virtually all assets subject the investor to purchasing power risk, since the realized return may be less than the rate of inflation. For example, when an individual investor purchases a fixed-income security such as a long-term corporate or municipal bond, the investor locks in a particular return. If inflation increases, the fixed return may be insufficient to compensate for the rate of inflation. Of course, if deflation occurs, the real purchasing power of the fixed return is increased.

An investor seeking to avoid loss of purchasing power should not acquire fixed-income securities but instead should buy variable-income securities. For example, the return earned on investments in money market mutual funds, money market bank accounts, or any short-term asset that is rapidly retired is not fixed. The rapid turnover of these assets permits yields to quickly adjust, allowing you to reinvest the funds at the higher short-term rates. Thus, these assets are among the best means to reduce purchasing power risk.

The diversity of alternative investments available to the individual investor should be immediately apparent from the summary on page 70. Obviously not all of these investments are appropriate to meet specific investment goals. Also, some of them would not be appropriate for someone like Joan Stuart with her extremely modest resources, or someone who is very averse to risk. Since each *Pre-REtirement Planner*'s financial resources, aversion to risk, and tax environment vary, there are many possible portfolios that different individuals can construct. Each portfolio, however, should seek to obtain the maximum possible return given the investor's resources and willingness to bear risk.

In addition, the investor must decide whether or not to manage the portfolio actively. Some of you *Pre-REtirement Planners* have neither the time nor the inclination to oversee your portfolios and thus employ the services of others—financial planners, stockbrokers, portfolio managers in trust departments, or the managers of mutual funds. However, individual investors must still select who will administer their assets and, of course, must suffer any losses that result from poor management of the funds. Ultimately it is the saver who bears the risk and reaps the reward from the portfolio, whether the funds are managed by himself or by others.

Various types of investments are listed in the summary of investment alternatives. The *Pre-REtirement Planner* may well be confused by the wide range of choices offered. We will now attempt to describe them in easy-to-follow terms.

Money or cash which has not been invested achieves no return. Thus the ''emergency fund'' hidden in the cookie jar *costs* the saver money through the loss of interest income.

NOW and savings accounts are federally insured (up to $100,000 for the account in a particular institution) and are accessible immediately by simply writing a check or personally withdrawing funds. Within the federal insurance limits, these investments are 100 percent safe, and earn interest at the lowest rates, often below the rate of inflation. Some banks offer money market savings accounts with slightly higher yields, but these usually require the maintenance of a minimum balance and limit the number of free checks or withdrawals, with high fees charged for additional withdrawals. If you tend to keep sums of cash on hand for emergencies, deposit them instead in one of these savings accounts. This should be your cookie jar!

Certificates of deposit (CDs) are also federally insured for up to $100,000 per depositor and are thus risk-free up to that amount. A minimum investment is usually required (sometimes as low as $500) for a minimum period such as ninety days. CDs are generally offered for much longer periods, at increasing interest rates, and may require higher minimum investments. The interest rates for CDs are higher than for savings and NOW accounts, as long as you do not redeem before they mature. If you have an emergency requiring such redemption, you will be penalized by receiving a lower rate of interest and may be charged a redemption fee.

Money market mutual funds offer shares in a pool of short-term money market instruments including bank certificates of deposit, corporate short-term borrowing (commercial paper), and U.S. Government securities (Treasury bills). While these investments are not insured, they are relatively risk-free because the money funds spread their investments among a large number of banks, major corporations, and various government agencies. These investments generally follow changes in interest rates and usually provide a slightly higher return than savings and NOW accounts. Shares of money market mutual funds are easy to redeem, and some funds provide checks so that an investor can draw on the investment at any time. There may be a minimum amount of at least $500 for such checks.

Quality corporate bonds are issued by corporations and sold in denominations of $1,000 each. The most common are (1) mortgage bonds, secured by real estate; (2) equipment trust certificates, secured by equipment; and (3) debentures, which are unsecured and therefore supported by the creditworthiness of the corporation. Bonds usually pay a fixed amount of interest and have a specified date of maturity, and they may be redeemable (callable) prior to maturity. Other types of bonds include convertible bonds, which may be converted into a certain number of shares of common stock of the corporation, and zero-coupon bonds. Zero-coupon bonds sell at a deeply discounted price from face value. The difference between the discounted price and the face value received at maturity is the interest earned on the bond. Corporate bonds are purchased through brokers, and prices fluctuate daily, reflecting changes in the level of interest rates.

All bonds have risk caused by changes in interest rates. Since the interest rate on a bond is usually fixed—say, 9 percent for a $1,000 bond maturing in the year 2000—changes in the level of interest rates will cause the price of the bond to fluctuate. For example, if interest rates increase to 10 percent, the $1,000 bond will sell at a discount, such as $900, so that the effective interest rate will meet the market. The interest of $90 which the corporation pays on this $1,000-face-value bond now represents 10 percent of the current discounted price of $900. The investor who paid face value for this bond would suffer a loss of $100 if the bond were sold for $900. On the other hand, if interest rates *decline,* the price of the bond will *increase.* In this case, an investor selling such a bond may realize a capital gain on the sale—the difference between the higher selling price and the original purchase price. The quality of corporate bonds is rated by Moody's Investors Service and Standard & Poor's Corporation. Quality corporate bonds generally receive a rating of A to AAA. The current ratings of a particular bond issue may change to reflect changes in the financial performance of the issuing corporation.

Interest earned on long-term corporate bonds tends to exceed interest earned on short-term investments; however, interest income will be fixed until the maturity of the bond, and the bond's price will fluctuate inversely with changes in interest rates. If you need cash for an emergency and have to sell bonds, you will have to sell for less than you paid if interest rates are higher than they were when you purchased the bond. Thus corporate bonds should be viewed as long-term investments that offer higher interest rates than money market mutual funds, but with additional risk should interest rates rise.

Federal tax laws require you to report interest income earned on bonds. This includes zero-coupon bonds; you must pay federal income taxes on the increase in the value even though the increase is not received until you sell their bond or redeem it at maturity. This disadvantage of owning zero-coupon bonds is eliminated if the bond is owned through a tax-deferred IRA, Keogh, or 401(k) plan. Then the tax on the accrued interest will be deferred until the funds are withdrawn.

Lower-rated corporate bonds pay higher interest but are riskier than quality corporate bonds. These have the same characteristics as quality corporate bonds except that they are riskier and receive lower ratings from Moody's and Standard & Poor's. That additional risk will result in a higher current interest rate, but could result in no interest payment in the future and possible loss of principal if the corporation defaults. Bonds rated Baa by Moody's and BBB by Standard & Poor are considered of medium grade and are more vulnerable to adverse economic conditions or changing circumstances. Bonds with lower ratings are considered speculative and thus have higher yields. There is also doubt about principal repayments at maturity.

While most *Pre-REtirement Planners* should avoid lower-rated bonds, those who have relatively large investment portfolios and are reasonably sophisticated investors may consider them. In recent years,

74

large quantities of "junk" bonds have been issued to finance takeovers and mergers. These are usually subordinated debentures and will often pay interest 3 or 4 full percentage points higher than quality bonds. Such bonds should be purchased only by those who can afford to lose their investment. Avoid "junk" bonds if your future retirement income depends on the interest income and safety of your principal.

Preferred stock pays a fixed dividend, thus providing, like bonds, a fixed flow of income. Lower yields are earned on quality preferred stock issued by strong or "blue-chip" companies. Higher yields are paid by weaker corporations. Preferred stock is part of the equity of a corporation and is not debt. While bonds must be retired at a specified time, preferred stock may have no maturity. Although preferred stock dividends must be paid before any common stock dividends, a corporation may omit or defer preferred stock dividends, while bondholders may take a corporation to court to collect unpaid interest.

Treasury bills are short-term federal government debt instruments. They are sold in denominations of $10,000 to $1,000,000 and mature in three to twelve months. "T-bills" may be purchased through commercial banks and brokerage firms and directly from Federal Reserve banks. They are sold at a discount from face value, the difference between the face value and the price being the interest. Treasury bills are virtually risk-free and produce yields comparable to money market mutual funds. There is an active secondary market in which the bills may be bought and sold. If you have less than $10,000 to invest, you may still participate in Treasury bills through the purchase of money market mutual funds which specialize in government securities.

Treasury bonds are long-term federal government debt instruments. They are issued in denominations of $1,000 to $1,000,000 and mature more than five years from the date of issue. Treasury bonds can be purchased in the same manner as Treasury bills. Because of their longer term, interest rates are usually higher than those paid by Treasury bills. As with any fixed income security, the market price of Treasury bonds will fluctuate inversely with changes in interest rates. Thus you could lose money on an investment in Treasury bonds if interest rates rise after you purchased the bond.

EE and HH bonds are nonmarketable federal government debt sold to individual investors. Series EE bonds sell at a discount. The smallest costs $25 with a face value of $50 and a guaranteed annual yield of 6 percent. The interest is the higher of 6 percent or 85 percent of the average rate on five-year Treasury securities. Thus, the purchaser of EE bonds is certain of a minimum yield of 6 percent if held to maturity and could earn a higher yield should interest rates rise. Federal income taxes on Series EE bonds may be deferred until they are redeemed (at a commercial bank) or mature. Series HH bonds are sold at face value (par) in denominations beginning with $500. HH bonds mature in ten years and pay 7½ percent interest to maturity. The interest is paid every year and is subject to federal income taxes. HH bonds are attractive to investors who require current income, while Series EE bonds appeal more to investors who do not require current income and want to increase the value of their investment by accumulating the tax-deferred interest.

Municipal bonds are exempt from federal income taxes and may be exempt from state and local income taxes. The interest rates paid on municipal debt are lower than those available on taxable bonds. Investors are willing to accept the lower interest rates on municipal bonds because of the tax exemption. For an investor in the 28 percent federal income tax bracket, a municipal bond yielding 5.76 percent per year in tax-exempt interest is equivalent to a corporate bond yielding 8 percent in taxable interest. Thus your marginal income tax and the yields on municipal and corporate bonds will determine whether or not tax-exempt municipal bonds are a sound investment for you. Investors considering municipal bonds should fully understand their personal income tax situation. Current tax laws may reduce the benefit of tax-exempt interest for wealthier taxpayers through the alternative minimum tax.

Like corporate bonds, municipal bonds vary in quality from relatively safe to relatively risky. Moody's and Standard & Poor's rating services evaluate municipal bonds based on the issuing government's ability to pay the interest and retire the principal. The ratings thus give you a reasonable indication of the risk associated with a particular issue. In addition, some bonds are insured, in which case quality of the insurance should improve the safety associated with the particular municipal bond.

Federal agency bonds are not debt of the federal government but are issued by various government agencies. Those agencies issuing long-term bonds include the Federal Home Loan Mortgage Corporation, the Government National Mortgage Association, and the Banks for Cooperatives organized under the Farm Credit Act. Some are secured by the U.S. Treasury and others have only "moral" backing by the federal government. However, these bonds have virtually no risk of default because the federal government would probably not permit the debt of one of its agencies to default. These bonds offer slightly higher yields than U.S. Treasury debt and are excellent investments for *Pre-REtirement Planners* looking for higher income with safety of principal.

Mortgage-backed securities are issued by the Government National Mortgage Association (Ginnie Mae) and the Federal Home Loan Mortgage Corporation (Freddie Mac). These securities are sold in denominations of $25,000 and may be purchased through commercial banks and stockbrokers. Investors may also purchase these bonds in more modest amounts by purchasing shares in mutual funds that specialize in federal agency debt.

Common stock represents equity (ownership) in a corporation. A share of common stock has no maturity date and is bought and sold on organized exchanges—for example, the New York Stock Exchange or American Stock Exchange, or in the informal over-the-counter market. Stocks are usually purchased through stockbrokers for a fee, which varies with the type of stockbroker. Full-service brokers who analyze and recommend common stocks charge higher fees than discount brokers who merely execute orders to buy or sell.

The price of stock depends on the corporation's earnings and dividends, the value of the underlying assets, and the firm's prospects for the future. The price of common stock is also affected by economic activity within the corporation's particular industry and by the economy as a whole. During periods of prosperity, stock prices in general rise, while during periods of slow economic growth or recession, prices fall.

The variety of firms that have issued common stock ranges from relatively low-risk conservative firms to high-risk speculative firms. Some quality stocks—for example, public utilities—may pay dividends at rates that are close to the yields on bonds. For the most part, however, dividend yields are lower than bond yields. Therefore, the opportunity to earn a reasonable return on an investment in common stocks requires price appreciation in addition to dividends. Speculative stocks generally pay no dividends. The entire return depends on price appreciation. Such stocks should be purchased only by sophisticated investors who can risk their entire investment.

Mutual funds are investment companies that sell their shares directly to the investor. Assets, such as stocks or bonds, are purchased with the funds these companies receive from the sale of their shares. The price of a mutual fund represents its net asset value (assets minus liabilities) plus a sales fee, called a "load," unless it's a "no load" fund, in which case there are no commissions. When investors want to sell their shares, the mutual fund redeems the shares at the then current net asset value. For many funds the sale involves no fee.

The original concept was for the mutual fund to purchase a diversified portfolio of assets (common stocks, bonds, U.S. Treasury securities, etc.) which would be managed by professionals. The purpose of the fund would be to produce both income and growth in principal through the construction of a diversified portfolio. That original objective has been modified by some mutual funds. Investors may now purchase shares in funds that specialize in growth common stock, gold (securities and commodities), government securities, high-technology stocks, or public utilities. Other mutual funds specialize in debt securities. *Pre-REtirement Planners* can acquire specialized bond funds with portfolios consisting of corporate bonds, federal government bonds, or tax-exempt securities.

While the portfolios of the specialized funds contain a variety of assets, the specialization tends to increase the risk. The benefits of diversification are reduced the more specialized the fund. As with investing in any asset, mutual funds should be purchased with care. Special attention should be given to past performance and to costs, which include the load fees, management fees, and other expenses. These costs can be substantial, and, of course, they reduce the return the investor earns.

6
Answering Your Questions

TAX-DEFERRED RETIREMENT PLANS

Q: What are the common tax-deferred retirement savings plans?

A: IRAs, Keogh plans, and 401(k) plans.

Q: What is an IRA?

A: An IRA (Individual Retirement Account) is a tax-deferred retirement account primarily for individual workers who are not covered by a pension plan where they work. These individuals may contribute up to $2,000 annually and deduct the contribution from their taxable income. If they earn less than $2,000, the maximum allowable contribution is the amount earned.

Q: May workers who are covered by a pension plan start an IRA?

A: Yes. However, there are constraints on the individual's ability to deduct the contribution from taxable income. If the individual earns less than $25,000 ($40,000 on a joint return), the contribution may be deducted. For incomes above those levels, the deduction is reduced by

$1 for every $5 adjusted gross income. Thus for a single individual earning $35,000 ($50,000 on a joint return), the deduction is completely phased out.

Q: If my income is over the amount that permits me to deduct the contribution, should I open an IRA?

A: This is not an easy question to answer because it depends on such factors as what other alternatives are available to you, such as a 401(k) plan and your capacity to save systematically. If funds are automatically transferred from another account to an IRA, that will help overcome a tendency to spend the funds and argues for an IRA even if you cannot deduct the contribution. If you are more disciplined, this forced saving may not be necessary. Another argument for an IRA—even if you can't deduct the contributions—is that the income earned by the account is tax-deferred until the funds are withdrawn from the account. The IRS requires you to report nondeductible contributions with your 1040 and the maximum contribution remains $2,000 annually.

Q: May I have a joint IRA with my spouse?

A: No. IRA stands for *Individual* Retirement Account.

Q: Am I allowed to take funds out of the account?

A: Yes, but if the withdrawal occurs before age 59½, you have to pay a penalty of 10 percent of the amount withdrawn as well as the federal income tax on the withdrawal. In cases of death and disability, withdrawals prior to 59½ are permitted without penalty. You must start to withdraw by April 1 after reaching the age of 70½

Q: What is the maximum amount I may withdraw at age 59½?

A: There is no maximum. You may withdraw all the funds at one time. However, you will owe federal income tax on the entire amount, so it is generally more advantageous to withdraw the funds over a period of time and continue to earn tax-deferred income.

Q: What is the minimum amount I may withdraw?

A: There is no minimum for withdrawals before age 70½. After that age, minimum withdrawals are based on your life expectancy. Since you may use your own and your spouse's life expectancy, the minimum required withdrawal varies among individuals. For example, the life expectancy of a 70½-year-old man and his 65-year-old wife is different from that of a 70½-year-old female and her 65-year-old husband. Hence the minimum amount that must be withdrawn by each saver would differ.

Q: What happens if I don't make the required withdrawals?

A: You will have to pay a penalty that is sufficiently large to induce you to make the required withdrawal.

Q: What is a Keogh account?

A: A Keogh account—also called an HR 10 plan—is a tax-deferred retirement plan for the self-employed.

Q: Can I open a Keogh account if I have a regular job and am covered by a pension?

A: Not unless you also have self-employed income, in which case you qualify for a Keogh.

Q: How much may I contribute?

A: If you have a basic money contribution plan instead of a profit-sharing plan, you may contribute a maximum of 20 percent of your income up to $30,000. For example, if you earned $20,000, you could contribute $4,000. You would also be eligible to contribute and deduct $2,000 for an IRA account, since you are under the thresholds that phase out the IRA deduction.

Q: Do contributions to a Keogh account reduce the amount of Social Security taxes I pay?

A: No. Contributions to IRA, Keogh, and 401(k) plans do not reduce Social Security taxes. It is income tax, not Social Security tax, that is deferred.

Q: What are the withdrawal requirements for Keogh accounts?

A: The same as for IRAs: a penalty for premature withdrawals before age 59½ and minimum required withdrawals based on life expectancy at age 70½.

Q: Are there any pitfalls in Keogh plans?

A: Yes. If you have employees, they must also be covered, provided they meet specified requirements such as age and length of service. You cannot just cover yourself. There are also more reporting requirements for Keogh plans. However, these disadvantages are offset by the obvious advantage that considerably more money may be contributed to a Keogh than to an IRA. So if you're eligible for a Keogh, it is more advantageous than an IRA.

Q: In what assets may I invest my Keogh and IRA funds?

A: The variety of assets ranges from savings accounts, stocks, bonds, and mutual funds to limited partnerships. There are, however, some assets that may not be held in these accounts, but these assets—for example, collectibles—are not generally appropriate as retirement vehicles anyway.

Q: I am not self-employed and earn too much to have an IRA and deduct the funds. Are there any other tax-deferred retirement plans?

A: Your employer may offer a salary reduction plan in which your salary is reduced and the funds placed in a retirement plan. While your total income is not altered, the retirement contribution comes off the top. It reduces your current taxable income and thus reduces your current taxes. For corporations, these plans are called 401(k) plans. Similar plans may also be available for employees of tax-exempt organizations and are referred to as 403(b) plans.

Q: Do employers have to offer these plans?

A: No, but they have become increasingly popular, and most firms of any size do offer them.

Q: How much can I contribute?

A: Contributions vary with the terms of the employer's plan. The maximum amount that you're allowed to contribute and deduct from income is 25 percent of compensation up to a maximum of $7,000. (This amount will be adjusted in the future for inflation.) Additional funds up to a total of $30,000 may be permitted in which case the contributions in excess of $7,000 are made with previously taxed dollars. Employers may choose to make matching contributions. Such matching funds should encourage the individual to make the maximum permissible contribution.

Q: Which plan is better, an IRA or a 401(k)?

A: The larger contribution favors the 401(k). Also, contributions to an IRA reduce the deductibility of contributions to your 401(k).

Q: Do I have any control over how the funds will be invested?

A: The answer may be both yes and no, depending on the options offered by the employer's plan. In many savings plans the employee is given several choices that may include a money fund, a common stock fund, a bond/fixed income fund, or a fund that invests solely in the common stock of the firm offering the plan. If such options are given, then the individual does have some control over how the funds are invested. You should be certain to ascertain from your employer what options are available.

Q: Which of the options is best?

A: There is no obvious and certain answer to this question. A money fund will be the least risky alternative but will offer the lowest return. Either a bond fund or a common stock fund should earn more. A fund limited to the stock of the employer is the most risky alternative, since your job and your retirement savings plan depend on the well-being of one firm. However, since you work for the firm, you may have some insight into its quality and potential for growth over a period of time. Also, most plans permit you to move funds among the available alternatives, so not all of the funds have to be invested in one option.

Q: What time scheme should I follow when choosing among investment alternatives such as those offered by a 401(k) plan?

A: Unless you're retiring in the relatively near future, retirement investing is long-term. You are not trying to catch swings in the financial markets. Investments in the securities of quality firms may be preferred, since over a long period of time such investments tend to offer returns that exceed both the rate of inflation and the return on short-term securities.

Q: What happens to the funds I have in a 401(k) plan if I leave the firm?

A: The funds are yours, and your options depend on the terms of your employer's plan. You may be permitted to leave your funds until age 65, in which case they will continue to grow, tax-deferred. If you take the funds, you have sixty days to roll them over into another tax-deferred account. If you do not roll over the funds within the sixty-day period, they become taxable income. Perhaps your easiest alternative is to establish an IRA rollover account with a bank, mutual fund, or brokerage firm. The tax then continues to be deferred.

Q: Suppose I decide to change my IRA account from a bank to a mutual fund. Is this allowed?

A: Yes, but only once a year. This is a good argument for investing IRA funds or IRA rollover accounts with an investment company that sponsors a variety of mutual funds. You may switch the money among the various funds as often as you wish. The once-a-year limit does not apply unless you switch from one financial institution's family of funds to another institution's family of funds.

Q: Is it possible to have more than one IRA account?

A: Yes. While it may not make sense to have $2,000 invested in one IRA account, $3,500 in a second, and $2,750 in a third, it does make sense to divide a substantial amount into more than one account. If you were to receive a $150,000 distribution from a savings plan, you could choose to break it into several IRA rollover accounts. For example, you might invest $50,000 in a FDIC-insured CD, $50,000 in a growth stock mutual fund, and $50,000 in a government securities fund. Such a strategy provides diversification as well as continuing to defer the federal income tax.

Q: Do employers offer any other savings programs?

A: Some employers allow employees to buy Treasury securities such as EE bonds through payroll deductions. There is a tax benefit from participation in that interest income can be tax-deferred until the bonds are cashed in or mature. Also the interest is not subject to city or state income taxes. These plans are a convenient means to save, because you can't spend money you haven't received unless you run up credit card balances, in which case you are only fooling yourself.

Q: Can I use life insurance to help finance retirement?

A: Yes, except with term insurance. Ordinary life, universal life, and variable life have savings components. You may borrow against the cash value and use the borrowed funds to help finance retirement. You should determine your need for insurance before using this strategy, however, since the death benefits are reduced by the amount you have borrowed. Another possibility is to use some of the cash value to buy a smaller paid-up policy and purchase an annuity or some other investment with the balance.

SOCIAL SECURITY

Q: Who may collect Social Security benefits?

A: Most individuals will have had to contribute—that is, pay Social Security taxes—for forty quarters to be eligible to receive benefits based on their own work record. However, you may be eligible to receive benefits based on someone else's work record without your having worked forty quarters.

Q: How are my benefits determined?

A: Social Security benefits depend on how long you have worked and how much you have contributed into the system. If you have contributed the maximum amount each year for thirty-five years, you could expect in 1989 to receive $899 monthly. If you contributed less than the maximum each year or worked for fewer than thirty-five years, your Social Security payment will be less. If you are approaching retirement, the Social Security Administration will estimate your monthly payment.

Q: I am a 50-year-old *Pre-REtirement Planner*. Is there any way I can estimate my Social Security benefits?

A: Since you are several years from retirement, any estimate may be tenuous at best. However, if you have been contributing the maximum each year and expect to continue to contribute the maximum, you can use the $899 as a starting point. Next, assume a rate of inflation, such as 5 percent. Multiply the $899 by the interest factor in Table 1, The Future Value of One Dollar, at 5 percent for fifteen years, as we did in chapter 2. The result, $1,869, would be the amount necessary to maintain the purchasing power of $899 after fifteen years if the rate of inflation is 5 percent. This answer, of course, assumes that Social Security benefits are not increased in real terms and that they will continue to be increased at the rate of inflation. Both of these assumptions seem reasonable. In this time of federal government budget deficits, it is doubtful that benefits will be increased by an amount that is greater than the rate of inflation.

Q: What happens to my Social Security payment if I retire early?

A: Benefits are reduced. You have to be 65 and retired to receive full benefits. At age 62 you will receive 80 percent of the benefit you would receive at age 65.

Q: Suppose I retire at 62. Do I have to start collecting benefits?

A: No. You may wait until you are older to start collecting.

Q: Is this advisable?

A: Not necessarily. While your annual benefits will be smaller if you start collecting at age 62, you have the immediate use of the money.

It will take many years for the higher payments at age 65 to offset the immediate use of the smaller payments.

Q: What happens to my Social Security payment if I retire after age 65?

A: Just as benefits are reduced if you retire early, they are increased if you retire later.

Q: Can I retire from one job, get another job, and collect Social Security payments?

A: The answer is yes, but there is a maximum income beyond which you will lose your Social Security benefits. If you are less than 65, you may earn $6,480 in 1989 before losing benefits. If you are 70 or older, you may earn any amount of income and not lose Social Security benefits.

Q: If I am 68 and earn $10,000, how much will I lose?

A: You lose $1 in benefits for every $2 earned over $8,800. Since your earned income exceeds $8,800 by $1,200, you will lose $600 in Social Security benefits. (In 1990 the law changes. You will lose $1 for every $3 earned, unless you are 70 or older, in which case you do not lose any benefits.) The loss of benefits is a strong argument against receiving Social Security benefits and continuing to work.

Q: How will Social Security know that my earned income exceeded $8,800?

A: You file forms with the Social Security Administration in much the same way you file income tax forms.

Q: Do other sources of income such as pensions, interest, dividends, capital gains, and rents and royalties reduce Social Security benefits?

A: No. It is only *earned* income that reduces benefits.

Q: Will my spouse receive benefits based on my work record?

A: Your spouse's benefits depend on his or her record or your record. If the spousal benefits are better under your record, then the spouse receives the higher benefit. For example, suppose a male has worked for 35 years and can expect to receive the maximum amount—$899 a month in 1989. His wife has worked outside the home for twelve years. She is thus eligible to receive benefits—that is, has worked more than forty quarters—but the benefits would be lower than she would receive based on her husband's work record. In that case, she would receive the higher amount because her benefits will be based on her husband's and not her own work record.

Q: It appears that the spouse has lost the benefits based on her work record. Is that true?

A: Yes. The spouse gets the higher of two possible benefits but not both.

Q: Is it possible for the husband's benefits to be based on his wife's work record?

A: Yes. Social Security benefits do not depend on gender.

Q: If I die, what happens to my Social Security benefits?

A: They are transferred to your spouse, provided that she or he is 60 years old and retired. Benefits may also be passed on to other dependents; check with Social Security to determine if that is applicable in your situation. If the spouse is less than 60, benefits will cease until the spouse reaches 60. If the spouse is working, then the limits on earned income discussed above apply. If the spouse is retired and collecting under his or her own record, the surviving spouse collects the higher of the two possible benefits but not both.

Q: If I retire and my spouse is less than 60 years old, should I consider life insurance?

A: Yes. It would be advantageous to have enough insurance to cover the period between your death and the point at which the spouse becomes eligible for Social Security benefits.

Q: Will my Social Security benefits be taxed?

A: That depends on your income from other sources. For most retirees Social Security benefits will not be taxed under current law. However, for about a quarter of recipients, up to half of their benefits will be taxed. If your adjusted gross income, plus your nontaxable income, plus one half of your Social Security payments is $25,000 ($32,000 for a couple filing jointly), your Social Security will be taxed. In the worst-case scenario, one half of your Social Security will be taxed at your tax bracket. Thus if your Social Security benefits are $10,000 and you're in the 28 percent income tax bracket, the maximum possible tax you will pay on Social Security benefits is $.28 \times \$5,000 = \$1,400$.

Q: How do I get Social Security benefits?

A: *You must apply for them.* Contact Social Security two to three months prior to your planned retirement and take your W-2 forms for the last three years, so that Social Security will have the most recent information on your contributions to Social Security. Benefits are distributed monthly and may be directly deposited to your bank account.

PENSION PLANS

Q: Do pension plans differ?

A: Yes. Pension plans are either defined contribution or defined benefit plans. As the name implies, in a defined contribution plan a specified percentage is contributed each year to the worker's pension account. A profit-sharing plan is illustrative of a defined contribution plan because the contribution is specified—that is, based on profits. Since the annual contributions vary as profits vary, the individual cannot be certain what the pension will be. With a defined benefit plan, the amount of the pension is specified. For example, the pension may be 50 percent of your final salary if you have worked for the firm for twenty-five years. Since you know your salary and how long you have worked for the firm, you should be able to estimate your potential pension.

Q: Do Social Security payments affect my pension payments?

A: That depends on your plan. Some pensions are in addition to Social Security payments while others are integrated with Social Security. If your pension is integrated, it is in effect a supplement to your Social Security payment. You should check with your employer's benefits division to determine your individual situation. You should also be given an estimate of your pension.

Q: Are pensions protected against inflation?

A: Generally they are not, although there are exceptions. If your pension is not inflation-protected, you will receive the same amount each year. Inflation will then erode the purchasing power of that flow of income, so it is important to have accumulated other assets to make up your pension's lost purchasing power.

Q: What are my pension choices when I retire?

A: Ask your employer. Usually the individual has several choices. These include a single series of payments, called an annuity, for the duration of the worker's life with all payments ceasing at the death of the employee. Other choices include an annuity for the life of the retiree and spouse or an annuity for the lifetime of the employee and two-thirds annuity for the surviving spouse. Other possibilities may include payments to children or other dependents.

Q: What effect will the selection of the distribution have on the amount?

A: Your employer will have set aside an amount to fund your pension. Your choice does not affect the amount of the fund but does affect its distribution. The longer the expected time over which the pension is to be paid, the smaller will be the individual payments. Thus if your spouse is 60 years old, your pension will be less than that of another individual worker whose spouse is 64 years old, assuming both of you select a pension of equal payments spread over the expected lives of both the husband and wife.

Q: Must I accept my employer's pension plan? Can I take my pension funds elsewhere?

A: That depends on the plan. In many cases you may not withdraw the funds. If you can take a lump sum distribution, you will have to find an alternative investment strategy. As with the distribution of funds from a 401(k) plan, you have sixty days to roll over the funds. Otherwise all the funds immediately become taxable as income. If you do have this option, you ought to have decided what you will do with the money prior to its receipt, for sixty days can pass rapidly while you're contemplating what to do with your funds.

Q: If I can take the money, should I?

A: That's a difficult question because the answer depends on who can provide you with a higher flow of income. You should obtain estimates from brokerage firms, insurance companies, mutual funds, and banks, and then compare what you may receive from these alternatives with your employer's pension.

Q: Could I manage my own pension?

A: Yes, if you are permitted to remove the funds and roll them over into an IRA rollover account. In that case you could have a self-directed pension. Of course, if you make poor investments and lose the funds, you have kissed your retirement funds goodbye.

Q: If I manage my own funds, what returns can I reasonably expect from my investments?

A: That depends on the type of investments you make. Historical studies of investment returns over a period of many years suggest that investments in short-term assets (money market mutual funds, Treasury bills, and certificates of deposit) offer a return that tracks the rate of inflation. Long-term securities have achieved higher returns. The common stocks of the major firms—that is, the largest firms in the Standard & Poor's 500 Stock Index—have earned a return of about 9 percent annually. Riskier stocks—by which we mean not the small stocks traded over the counter but the 100 smallest firms in the S&P 500—have yielded 12 percent annually. These results suggest that you cannot expect to earn returns of 15 to 20 percent annually over an extended period of time and that you should avoid investments that claim to offer such returns. Remember: these are retirement funds and should not be subject to too much risk.

Q: Should I diversify?

A: Diversification is exceedingly important. Even if you are not managing your pension, you are still managing your portfolio of assets, which includes your pension. Diversify your assets so that the portfolio includes a variety of types of assets—for example, money market securities, stocks, bonds, and real estate. Perhaps the strongest argument for acquiring the shares of mutual funds is the diversification they offer. While it is unlikely that the typical mutual fund will beat the market over an extended period of time (especially when you consider selling expenses, management fees, and commissions, which reduce the stockholder's return), mutual funds do construct diversified portfolios. Thus the individual who buys the fund's shares obtains a claim on a diversified portfolio.

Part 2

PLANNING FOR YOUR PERSONAL
WELL-BEING

7

Second Careers

MANAGEMENT OF TIME

One thing is certain at the moment of retirement: the retiree will receive gifts. There are golf balls for those long-anticipated games on weekdays when the course won't be nearly so crowded as on the weekends you've had to settle for during all your working years. There are fly-tying kits to help you catch the wily fish hiding among the rocks of your favorite fishing hole. There are books to be read for pleasure instead of professionally—the mysteries, romances, and biographies you rarely had a chance to read while you were struggling to make a living and to enhance your career. The biggest gift of all, though, is a universal one that all retirees receive, without exception: the gift of time.

Do you *Pre-REtirement Planners* have any notion how much time will be yours when you retire? Let's use a simple mathematical formula. Taking as our model the basic forty-hour work week (eight hours a day, five days a week), and omitting vacation and overtime, multiply forty hours by fifty-two weeks, and then multiply that total by twenty-one years—assuming that as an average tenure. The total is 43,680 working hours, which we will label as "structured time." Time when your employer expects you to be on the job.

Now compare that figure with only ten years of retirement. Your eight-hour day is now total waking time: twelve hours. You are suddenly responsible not only for weekends but for the entire seven-day week. Hence, we have a twelve-hour day multiplied by seven days times fifty-two weeks times ten years in retirement—a total of 43,680 hours! And this gift of time is totally unstructured.

These numbers are conservative, for most of us have more than twelve waking hours a day that must be shaped in some productive fashion. And how you decide to structure your new time is entirely up to you. There will be no boss to give you direction, no table of organization to fit neatly into. You are on your own. You are now your own time manager.

Your first reaction may be: "But why put structure into my life? This is exactly what I've been looking forward to—a chance to do what I want to do when I want to do it. No more boss noticing when I come in or leave. No meetings at a certain hour. No one looking over my shoulder. Finally I'm my *own* boss."

And so you are. The master of every minute; a clean slate to be filled only with what *you* decide will go there. But time is only a gift if one manages it wisely. Let's see if we can determine as precisely as possible what you will do with this new and generous allotment of time. The first step is to fill in the worksheet titled Typical Pre-Retirement Week Schedule, which plots your time as it is spent now. Next, after taking some time to think it out, complete the next worksheet, Typical Week's Schedule After Retirement, which sketches a plan of what you intend to include in your daily activities after you leave the job. This will require an exercise of imagination and projection, because chances are you have never before had such a blank check of free hours—one that you can fill in with any number that pleases you.

Finally, return to both the pre-retirement schedule and the retirement schedule and circle those activities that you share with your spouse, friends, or relatives. Most of you will note a vast difference between the time you now spend with your mate (not all that much) with the time contemplated in retirement (a great deal!). The majority of *Pre-REtirement Planners* have told us they spend much more time with their colleagues than with their families. Unless you deliberately diversify your activities, you can expect a similar change after retirement.

TYPICAL PRE-RETIREMENT WEEK SCHEDULE

Hour	Sunday	Monday	Tuesday	Wednesday	Thursday	Friday	Saturday
5 A.M.							
6 A.M.							
7 A.M.							
8 A.M.							
9 A.M.							
10 A.M.							
11 A.M.							
12 Noon							
1 P.M.							
2 P.M.							
3 P.M.							
4 P.M.							
5 P.M.							
6 P.M.							
7 P.M.							
8 P.M.							
9 P.M.							
10 P.M.							
11 P.M.							
12 Midnight							

TYPICAL WEEK'S SCHEDULE AFTER RETIREMENT

Hour	Sunday	Monday	Tuesday	Wednesday	Thursday	Friday	Saturday
5 A.M.							
6 A.M.							
7 A.M.							
8 A.M.							
9 A.M.							
10 A.M.							
11 A.M.							
12 Noon							
1 P.M.							
2 P.M.							
3 P.M.							
4 P.M.							
5 P.M.							
6 P.M.							
7 P.M.							
8 P.M.							
9 P.M.							
10 P.M.							
11 P.M.							
12 Midnight							

Two major areas are worth consideration: a second career, and volunteerism. Let's look at what a second career is all about. Many *Pre-REtirement Planners* assert, ''If I wanted to keep working I'd stay with my present job.'' But an important fact to learn is that work is different when you retire, and in some significant ways more satisfying. While you're on the job, you are aware that your performance is being monitored. Certain inevitable questions tend to make the job stressful. Will you get a promotion? Will you get a raise? Will your annual evaluation be a positive one? Climbing the corporate ladder can be an exhausting and difficult experience. But by retirement, usually we have reached the peak of our climb, and while the desire to do a good job will remain—and we will certainly appreciate our second-career salary—the career path is bound to be a lot less steep and worrisome.

For example, you may decide to take a job clerking for a major book chain. Unless you're the type who automatically makes molehills into mountains, you should be able to do the job without undue stress. You will not be overly concerned whether a certain title is in stock or not, or whether the store is willing to accept single-copy orders. You will not be responsible to shareholders for a big return on their investment. You will not be corporate-ladder climbing. If you grow weary of the job, there's no long-term commitment, no pension that you're trying to attain. In short, you are a free agent who can go or stay as you wish. If you care to, of course, you can make the job a stepping-stone to a bigger opportunity, but the choice is yours.

One advantage of working after retirement is that it offers us the socialization we were accustomed to in our pre-retirement years. Having to be on the job gives us a reason to get up in the morning, to keep ourselves properly groomed and garbed. Voltaire's statement that ''work spares us from three great evils—boredom, vice, and need'' is a truth not to be dismissed. Boredom and need are clearly understood problems, but what about vice? The vice might easily be an overindulgence in alcohol. Either from depression or from having no meetings or appointments to keep, some retirees have a couple of cocktails at lunch and nap away part of the afternoon. If you are committed to either a paid position or a volunteer function, the possibility that you'll overindulge is lessened.

A second career exposes us to a mixed age group, preventing our gravitating only to our contemporaries in a retirement setting. It helps us to relate to the real world and not isolate ourselves with one generation. Isolation is a serious problem for many people in retirement, and well before you retire you should begin to ask yourself the following questions: Do I have friends or interests outside my work? Do I reach out beyond my job and work friends to my family and community? If your answer to both questions is no, you may face extreme isolation in retirement.

How many of your business friends who have retired or transferred to another part of the organization do you still count as close friends? It is natural to drift away, almost imperceptibly and surely without intent, from colleagues with whom we have shared so much over the span of a career. The things you shared—the job itself, office politics, and other office friends—are no longer there. If you live in a small community perhaps these relationships can be maintained, but in large metropolitan areas where your common meeting place is the office or plant, you have to develop the friendship beyond work by visiting each other's homes and making an effort to meet on a regular basis.

Give yourself this test about such friendships. If you want to share some information with a fellow worker whom you consider a friend and you happen to think about it on a weekend, do you find yourself saying, ''I'll wait until Monday. I don't want to bother her (or him) at home''? If that is your response, the person is merely a business friend and one you will probably leave behind when the job is over.

WORKING PART-TIME

The pay in part-time work is usually low, but adding that salary to your Social Security benefit and pension, if there is one, can make the difference between a minimally acceptable life-style and maintaining the level you enjoyed in pre-retirement. If your income does not provide a safe cushion in relation to your expenses, which you determined from the financial worksheets, both spouses can earn up to the maximum allowed by the Social Security rules and thus create a comfortable retirement formula.

Where is the first place we tend to go when looking for a job, either part- or full-time? Most of us will turn to the classified section of the newspaper. But the best jobs—particularly those that are part-time or temporary—may not be advertised. Why not use a little creativity and try to custom-make one just for you? In *Modern Maturity* (August-September 1981), one woman told of how she obtained a part-time chef position and solved a restaurateur's problem simultaneously. Customers had been walking out because of poor service, the manager was overworked, and the cooks were constantly quitting. The author suggested a series of part-time cooks, starting with herself. Three retired women on three-hour shifts turned the business around.

A former CBS employee who liked to shop at Bloomingdale's decided that it would be fun to work there in retirement. She walked in and talked herself into an afternoon job in the gift-wrapping section. She loved working with young people. She learned what they were thinking and saying, what some of their problems and ambitions were. At the same time, she no longer had the old work pressure. She was free of the burden of performance appraisals and promotions, that big increase in pay that not only would pay for Johnny's tuition next fall but would show her that she was properly appreciated. Work takes on an entirely different meaning when you don't have to carve out a career and constantly take job worries home with you. The Bloomingdale's lady is now working to have fun and to mix with a variety of people, not to be Mrs. Career Superstar.

One CBS early retiree went from his upper management position to one quite different from anything he had ever done before. Tiring of time on his hands, this self-confident fellow took delight in making sandwiches in a delicatessen in his fashionable suburban town. At first his spouse was unenthusiastic about this change in status, but she came to understand that it met many of his needs in retirement. The story does not end there either: after learning the food business, he went ahead and bought his own delicatessen!

Another example of how to make your own career is provided by the ''Popcorn Professor,'' a recently retired professor from Simmons College in Boston, who decided he wanted a change from the academic scene. After researching several possibilities, he opened a popcorn stand in Boston's Faneuil Hall and hired a friend who wanted to separate himself from the banking business. They made their own hours; they worked only if the temperature outdoors was comfortable. The work was ideal for the Popcorn Professor's needs: he made a certain amount of money, he spent his hours out in the sun, and he met a wide variety of people each day, thereby fulfilling his sociability needs. And best of all, he was never bored.

Making such a drastic change in one's field might have been easy for the Popcorn Professor, but a transition from Ph.D. to street vendor could well prove difficult for many of us. If we don't have a strong sense of who we are and don't feel self-confident, this move from prestigious head of a college department to bagging popcorn might not work. However, if we can overcome obstacles of ego we might not consider it beneath our dignity to work at a job that is not as high on the ladder as our previous lifetime position. The need to be considered useful and wanted can be met by a lower-level job.

You may want to look for part-time work in a sport or a hobby. Frank Muoio, retired CBS engineer, teaches golf in his backyard, utilizing a television camera in the lesson. One of Muoio's job benefits is the constant physical exercise involved in instructing others. Tony Boschetti, another retired CBS employee, makes television commercials. Since his retirement he has appeared in bit parts in more than twenty movies and TV soap operas, working with, among others, Woody Allen and Dudley Moore.

Wes Vernon, a CBS Washington correspondent, has a stake in the *American Zephyr,* a two-car railroad train consisting of a lounge car and dining car which schedules weekend getaway trips, in-station parties, and special party excursions to major sporting events. This he is doing while still an active employee, following the PREP seminar motto: Do It Now!

WORKING FULL-TIME

Some new retirees, however, will want to find another full-time position, or will be forced to do so by economic pressures, in either the same or an allied field. It is important that *Pre-REtirement Planners* take courses or seminars to bring them up to date *while still working.* Also, consciously and conscientiously, they should begin to network, for strong professional contacts can be crucial to success. Knowledge of the job and skill on the job are not always the keys to finding employment;

for the retiree it is more often *who* you know, not *what* you know. So start making a list of personal contacts. Let them know that you're looking for a job. When you talk to someone you sense can be helpful, make sure to get that person's name and phone number. Have cards printed up and give them out liberally. Use—but don't abuse—those who can help you in your search. Get them to make telephone calls on your behalf, or to write recommendations.

Remember, you have many years of experience to sell; don't ever underestimate your importance. Very likely your skills are transferable to a new field. When CBS closed its guitar plant, there was a man whose job was finishing the wood on the neck of guitars. You can't get much more specialized than that. His chances of finding a similar job in another company were slim to nonexistent. But this man knew wood and how to work with it. He jumped from the guitar business to cabinet making, and in retirement he has more jobs than he can handle. The smartest move he made after retirement was to assess his strengths; he didn't waste time trying to find a job that would be the mirror image of the one he'd had for thirty years.

Many of those who are forced into early retirement try to find the same job in a similar company. It is a mistake to limit your horizons that drastically. It will prove much more practical and profitable to use your skills in a new context as the guitar finisher did, or else to go on to a field altogether new. As a *Pre-REtirement Planner*, think of an area that interests you, that you always wanted to become involved in, and if it is reasonably within your competence, learn to do it.

AGE DISCRIMINATION

All right, you say, it's fine to learn all the ins and outs of getting a job. But who will want me? When they see my gray hair and wrinkles I won't be given the job.

The trap in that response is that we may use age discrimination as the catchall reason for not obtaining a position, full- *or* part-time. Have we presented ourselves in a positive manner, proving that we would be an asset to that organization? Do we have the skills or talents necessary for the position to be filled? We didn't get every job we applied for when we were younger, so why should we expect to now? Age discrimination, of course, will always exist, just as other prejudices will, but if we use that reason without careful, honest self-evaluation, we will never get the job we want. If we run into problems, rather than blame it on our age we should check our skills, appearance, and attitudes to determine if the fault might not lie within ourselves.

USING YOUR SOURCES

If you have definitely decided on a second career, whether part- or full-time, it is now time for you to address four specific questions:

• How much do you want to make? Remember the limit if you're collecting Social Security.

• How many hours do you plan to work? Consider what other things you may want to enjoy in retirement and try to balance your priorities.

• How far are you willing to travel?

• How much responsibility are you prepared to take on?

Once armed with this personal data, decide if temporary, or permanent, part-time or full-time work best meets your needs and then attack your sources accordingly.

There are many places to look for part-time work. Consider your school placement offices, your union office, your college alumni bulletin. Every type of job has some kind of organization that will help place you. Tap those resources, and, as already pointed out, don't neglect your personal contacts. They can help, especially with jobs that are not advertised. Someone within an organization might know that a new department is opening up or that someone is going to leave or retire; many excellent jobs never reach the classifieds. Pursuing the hidden job market is a must.

Résumés are important, and yet many personnel people don't like to read them. Although you must have one, the best strategy is to withhold it until it's practically snatched out of your hands. A résumé is an easy way to get turned down. A company may be looking for someone with a master's degree in science and ten years of experience. You have forty years of experience but only a bachelor's degree; hence you've disqualified yourself before you had a chance to put a foot in the door. It is crucial to get in there and make your impression *before* your résumé is read.

Far more effective than a résumé is a letter to someone in a company you'd like to work for, explaining why you want to work for the company and what you can contribute. This letter should be addressed by name to the head of the department in which you want to be placed. If company literature does not contain the person's name, the switchboard operator will usually supply it. Explain a little about your background but only enough to pique his or her interest. Your objective is to be called in for an interview because that is where you have the greatest opportunity to sell yourself face-to-face; that's where you get the job. Mention in your letter that you will telephone next week if you have not heard from the department head in the interim. This will allow you to follow up with a phone call, remind him of your letter, and possibly set up an appointment.

First you must have the skills and talent that go with the position. But simply sending out reams of résumés will get you nowhere. However, when one is requested, be sure to deliver it personally. That way, someone may say, "You know, the person who came in here today seemed very nice." Already you have an edge.

STARTING YOUR OWN BUSINESS

If you're thinking of going into business for yourself, get in touch with SCORE—the Service Corps of Retired Executives. SCORE will provide you with a mentor who knows about the area that interests you, help you to set up your books, and keep you from falling into all of those potholes you don't even know exist. SCORE is free of charge and can make the difference between success and failure.

In many cases you're going to be putting up your own money. All the more reason to determine as clearly as possible at the outset whether or not that business is a good risk.

Dun & Bradstreet reports that in 1986, 252,532 small businesses (twenty or fewer employees) started up; 61,606 failed. In 1987, 235,187 started; 61,209 failed. According to *The State of Small Business: A Report of the President Transmitted to the Congress, March 1983,* ''Businesses under 5 years old account for 50 percent of the failures; 30 percent are 6–10 years old, and the remaining 20 percent are over 10 years old.''

The March 1984 issue of the same publication discusses the positive contributions made by independent small businesses to job generation and job retention. A serious entrepreneur would be well advised to order the latest issue of this report from the Superintendent of Documents, U.S. Government Printing Office, Washington, D.C. 20402, and study both risk and success ratios for any anticipated venture.

Most failed start-up operations don't have the benefit of sound advice; also, most of them have limited financial staying power. Surely you have seen a small store, new to the location, and said to yourself, ''I'm going to stop in there soon,'' and by the time you get around there again the place is empty and for rent.

It is a great American ideal to work for ourselves, but a difficult thing to accomplish. Think it out very carefully before embarking on any business venture. And use your imagination. For instance, zoning permitting the use of your home as a bed and breakfast business is a possibility.

Franchising is also an expensive proposition, but there are many successful ones. You can franchise Century 21, McDonald's, funeral parlors, and automobile agencies, to name only a few. There is a franchise for just about everything. Anyone interested in franchising should write to:

International Franchise Association
1350 New York Avenue N.W.
Suite 900
Washington, DC 20005
(Phone: 202-628-8000)

Publishes *IFA Directory of Membership* (more than a directory; much more information), *Investigate Before Investing* (helps evaluate franchise offerings), and *Is Franchising for You?*

Venture Magazine, Inc.
521 Fifth Avenue
New York, NY 10175-0028
(Phone: 212-682-7373)

Venture, a monthly magazine, identifying itself as a
publication ''For entrepreneurial Business Owners and
Investors,'' features a wide variety of articles on the
whole franchising scene.

Remember: When it comes to choosing a second career, you are
limited only by your own energy and ideas. Try to find a need, a niche,
and fill it. Look for—or create—a job you can put your whole heart into.
Be innovative and win!

8
Leisure Time

ACCENTUATE THE POSITIVE

Not many of us have had successful retirees as role models. Instead we have seen too many people mark time in old age; retired couples growing old before their time without goals or projects or any real interests; somewhat pathetic people exuding an air of aimlessness. For that reason, vast numbers of people fear the prospect of retirement and dread the "promise" of leisure time. It is important that as a *Pre-REtirement Planner* you guard against such negativism and rid yourself of the false and unfair impression that leisure equals nothingness. In reality, leisure time can provide many positive opportunities, among them the following:

• *Achieving growth,* by furthering your education, adding to your store of knowledge, and keeping your mind alive and active.

• *Shaping up,* by maintaining your body for both mental and physical health.

• *Being creative,* by letting your latent talents flower in such pursuits as painting, writing, and gardening, to name only three.

• *Being of service,* by directing your energies in the community.

• *Seeking pleasure,* by fulfilling some of your fondest dreams—for example, for travel—just for the sheer joy of it. After all, haven't thirty years of work earned you that right?

• *Finding self-esteem,* by replacing on-the-job recognition with personal achievement through any or all of the above activities.

TRAVEL

For retirees who are no longer limited to time or season, travel opportunities abound. Lower prices in the off-season are available, and airlines should be checked for their "senior specials." However, the timeworn caveat remains: if the package seems too good to be true, examine it with a critical eye before making a commitment. Find out how much walking or climbing will be required, if special diets can be accommodated, how quickly one moves from one location to another, and how much free time is planned in the schedule. Also check cancellation clauses and trip insurance coverage in the event of emergency changes in the plan.

For those who seek an unusual travel experience, Elderhostel, an educational program that combines both domestic and international travel with intellectual activity, might well be the answer. Its popularity is growing within the retiree population. Launched in 1975, this organization utilizes more than 1,000 colleges, universities, and other educational institutions in offering one-week, three-course programs for individuals 60 years of age and older. Spouses and companions who are at least 50 are welcome to accompany the primary person. Programs begin on Sunday afternoon and end the following Saturday morning. Lodgings in dormitories are simple and comfortable, all meals are provided, and bathroom facilities are usually shared rather than private. Since the courses are not for credit, there are no exams, and this allows a wide range of participants from Ph.D.s to those who have not finished high school. Elderhostel is an inexpensive combination of travel, education, and a means of widening your social horizons. The address: Elderhostel, 80 Boylston St., Suite 400, Boston, MA 02116.

Interhostel, conceived by the University of New Hampshire, also presents an exciting challenge for many new retirees. Describing itself as providing "a unique international study-travel experience," Interhostel is a fourteen-day program designed for adults 50 and older with a minimum age of 40 for a traveling companion. Twenty-four destinations throughout Europe and Asia are currently available. Each program features seminars or lectures taught in English, sightseeing and field trips, social activities, and lodging and meals. The topics usually include the nation's history, politics, economy, literature, arts, and music. Lodging is most often in college or university residence halls or modest hotels. The address: University of New Hampshire, Interhostel, 6 Garrison Avenue, Durham, NH 03824.

Check your health insurance before going to a foreign country, mindful that Medicare does not cover you there. You may want to call or write to the following organizations:

Access America
600 Third Avenue
New York, NY 10016
(Phone: 800-851-2800)

Travel Insurance Programs Corporation
243 Church Street West
Vienna, VA 22180
(Phone: 800-237-6615; in Virginia, 703-281-9500)

For a directory of English-speaking doctors around the world, get in touch with:

International Association of Medical Assistance to
Travelers (IAMAT)
417 Center Street
Lewiston, NY 14092
(Phone: 716-754-4883)

With this directory at hand, you can call a twenty-four-hour emergency number and be certain you will reach a doctor with whom you can communicate.

TRANSPORTATION TIPS

If traveling by train: Amtrak, the national rail system, offers a variety of discounts, excursions, escorted tours, and family discount plans. You can also get package plans including accommodations, transfers, and sightseeing. For further information write to Amtrak, 955 L'Enfant Plaza, Washington, DC 20024.

If traveling by ship: Many steamship lines have air/cruise arrangements so that you can sail to your destination and fly home. The majority of cruise ships offer dancing, golf, art classes, bridge, fashion shows, concerts, and calisthenics. You new retirees will find plenty of companionship aboard. Often senior groups or seniors traveling together are eligible for standby discount fares.

If traveling by air: Air fares change constantly. There is no way to predict what bargains may be available when you plan to fly, but generally you get the best bargains on package deals (most of which include air fare, hotel accommodations, meals, ground transportation, and sightseeing), advance-plan fares (for which you sign up sixty to ninety days in advance of your flight), or charter flights (for which you must belong to a group). Find out about legitimate charter flights by sending for a copy of *Air Travelers Fly-Rights,* free from the Office of Consumer Advocate, Civil Aeronautics Board.

If traveling by bus: Greyhound and Trailways offer books of tickets allowing unlimited travel for specified lengths of time. You can take tours throughout Europe by Europabus, which has English-speaking hostesses. For further information: Europabus, 11 East 44th Street, New York, NY 10017; Casser Tours, 201 West 41st St., New York, NY 10039; and American Express, Cooks, Tauck Tours, 475 Fifth Avenue, New York, NY 11107.

If traveling by automobile: Major oil companies will provide free maps and advice (Exxon Touring Services is located at P.O. Box 307, Florham Park, NJ 07932). Many budget motels are listed in *National Directory of Budget Motels,* available for $2.50 from Pilot Books, 347 Fifth Avenue, New York, NY 10016.

If you are 65 or older, apply for a free-entry Golden Age Passport at entrances to national parks and recreation areas; you may also get discounts on camping facilities. If you're interested in out-of-the-way

U.S. vacations, send for *Farm, Ranch & Countryside Guide* or *Adventure Guide,* both available from Adventure Guides, Inc., 36 East 57th Street, New York, NY 10022.

VOLUNTEERISM

In a quest for balance, the new retiree should consider contributing time to one or another worthy cause. Churches, schools, hospitals, and cultural groups are constantly seeking interested people who will volunteer their services. One of the most visible is Meals on Wheels, which depends on volunteers to deliver meals to the homebound. Many drivers assist the sick and elderly in keeping medical appointments. Hospital volunteers operate thrift shops and help both patients and their families. By helping those in need, many retirees experience a sense of joy and fulfillment that they never had in their careers.

Terri Wilburn retired from CBS five years ago to be home with her ailing husband, Howard. Unfortunately, Howard died about six months after her retirement, leaving her alone and without resources. Since then she has made a new life for herself. Not only has she learned to drive a car but she has taken an auto mechanics class so that she can know what's going on under the hood if necessary. Terri also joined the Roselle (New Jersey) Swim Club and learned to tread water at depths over her head, something she would never have dared doing when she was younger. In addition, Terri volunteers her time one day a week to the Memorial General Hospital Guild. Still not finished structuring her time, she creates silk flower arrangements and dolls made of wool, which she donates to worthy causes. Terri attributes her positive approach to her religious faith, saying that her belief in God inspires her to live life fully and joyfully, thereby helping herself as well as others.

A swim group in New Jersey, composed of retirees, is assisting arthritis victims in water exercises to relieve pain and maintain flexibility. A previous group there helped multiple sclerosis victims. There are many opportunities to serve in your community. Instead of waiting for someone else to meet a personal or collective need, why not go ahead and become the organizer yourself? We tend to think that someone else can do it better, that we might fail, that it might take too much time or money. There is always a sound "rational" reason *not* to do something. But if we can overcome the fear of failure and prod ourselves out of inertia, it's possible to accomplish worthwhile, even noble, deeds.

While we are pursuing a career and raising a family, with all the effort and time required, there is precious little time left over to volunteer and organize to help others. There are those who are serving, however, while we are working, and now, in retirement, perhaps our time to contribute has come.

A story used in PREP seminars reflects on this point. It concerns an old man who is planting a sapling on the front lawn of his house. A young fellow passes by, stops, watches the old man dig, and asks what he's doing. "Planting a peach tree," the old man replies. Puzzled by this, the young man says, "I don't mean to sound brash, but it takes many years for a small tree like the one you're planting to bear fruit. Do you really expect to eat fruit from this tree?" Rather than showing annoyance at the question, the old man answers, "Probably not, but I've been eating fruit all my life from trees other people planted. Maybe it's my turn to plant a tree." Perhaps our desire to volunteer our time in retirement grows out of just that philosophy.

EDUCATION

Retirement offers us the time and potential to grow. Continuing one's education either for a degree or simply for the opportunity to learn is an idea whose time has come. According to an article in the *New York Times,* November 12, 1987, gray hair on the campus is the new look. The City University of New York (CUNY) in 1986 had over 2,000 students 65 and over, double the number that age in 1980. As explained later, in Chapter 12, the left hemisphere of the brain—our logical side—actually *increases* its efficiency as we grow older. Armed with that assurance, don't be afraid to tackle courses in Irish literature, calculus, anthropology, or whatever interests you.

Attending college while still working is possible not only in night classes but at weekend colleges. If you are still working and your company has an education assistance program, why not get a jump ahead on retirement education now and continue it into retirement? A

CBS retired executive vice-president returned to a state college, earned an additional degree, and is currently spearheading a fund-raising drive for that institution. As he put it, he wasn't interested in learning more about his former specialty; instead, he chose classes that satisfied interests long set aside for the sake of business.

Getting the long-desired education is one way of "slaying the dragon" in your life. Another dragon could be a fear of flying that prevents your taking trips to faraway places you always dreamed of visiting. It could be a fear of water that keeps you from enjoying a swimming pool or the beach in summer. Or fear of driving a car, leaving you immobile and at the mercy of family, friends, or public transportation. Perhaps you can say to yourself, "I've always wanted to ———," and fill in the blank, or blanks, then begin to sort out why you haven't done those things you want to do and determine a way to make them happen. Pick a time; make a commitment; begin! You will feel the deep satisfaction of having educated yourself to a new stage of growth.

But, you say, my goal was to be a ballet dancer, and now at my age and physical condition it's too late. Let's modify the ambition, then, and set some goals that center around the art of dance. If you don't already attend the ballet, begin to do so. Read all you can about the art and the artist, past and present. There is a big world that surrounds the art of dance—the music, costuming, photographs, and paintings. Join that world as a part-time worker, a volunteer, or an amateur lover of the art.

SOME PERILS OF LEISURE TIME

Now a word of caution. Changes in relationships with spouse, children, and other family are almost inevitable when you retire. If your job has been outside the house, the amount of togetherness suddenly thrust on you can be stifling. It can be a test of patience and love. Suddenly time spent at home can create unexpected tensions, and leisure time, which you looked forward to all these years, can develop a bitter taste.

Over the years, married couples develop their own—and separate—schedules. Come retirement, that schedule must be reworked to make it satisfactory to both. Take the simple matter of lunch habits, for instance.

The newly retired person is accustomed to having lunch with business associates in restaurants. The spouse has been on a completely different schedule—housework, club meetings, and social gatherings at specified times. Now this new, unfamiliar coalition must work out a structure suitable for both. This will require honest communication of each other's needs, and it may not be so simple as it sounds. How does a loving spouse tell a mate that he or she is underfoot too much, is interfering or demanding? The person at home has been ''unsupervised'' until now and is hardly ready to relinquish that independence. One such woman told me her husband was used to having a secretary make his phone calls and generally be at his beck and call. He looked on his wife as a natural successor, a role she resented. Since he refuses to forgo the businessman routine totally, setting up his own home office and telephone answering service has made life simpler for them both.

There are situations and reactions that people cannot anticipate. A certain uneasiness, if not outright guilt, can result from secretly resenting having one's life changed as the result of retirement. A spouse's thoughts might run something like this: ''I should be happy to have John home all day. He's worked so hard through the years, paying the mortgage, putting the kids through college. He deserves to be out of the rat race. And what do I do? Feel sorry for myself because he interferes and tries to change my life.'' Such problems must be discussed frankly or the strains on the relationship can become intolerable.

9

A Place to Live

Jimmy Durante once said, "Did you ever get the feeling that you wanted to go and still have the feeling that you wanted to stay?" To stay or not to stay is the key question that many *Pre-REtirement Planners* have to deal with and often try to answer too quickly. As we Americans have become increasingly a nation of travelers, there is a temptation to sell the pre-retirement home and move to places we have lived in and loved for three weeks on vacation; and today, whether your projected retirement budget is upscale or modest, there seems an almost endless variety of choices open to you. You must analyze carefully the pros and cons of moving. If relocation proves to be a mistake, it's a difficult one to undo.

Some *Pre-REtirement Planners* dream of living on their own boat in the Caribbean and making extra income from chartering. Others have their hearts set on keeping bees or breeding dogs; still others may want to live in a mobile home, a residential hotel, or an adult community. Your retirement ideal may be to live by the sea, in the mountains, or at the desert. But precisely because there *are* so many choices—and because a mistake might prove costly—this is clearly a retirement decision to be made with caution. It is important to keep in mind that retirement is not a permanent vacation: it is still real life and you are still a real person, not that person portrayed in commercials and advertisements as perpetually riding in a golf cart on a bright, sunny day, hopping out and holing an eighteen-foot putt.

One recently retired woman told us, speaking for herself and her spouse: ''The point of view changes after retirement, and suddenly becomes more realistic. What seemed like a great romantic dream while working is not at all what we feel we want now.'' She went on to say: ''I would certainly advise all retirees who are thinking of moving to give several places a lot of thought, and don't decide in a hurry. You should take at least a year.''

Another *Pre-REtirement Planner* we'll call Diane had lived with her mother for a number of years in a once proud but recently decaying section of the Bronx. In the first flush of excitement attendant on her retirement, she found a lovely, airy, and secure apartment for them in Bergen County, New Jersey. It was a big step up—clean, roach-free, safe, and with access to senior citizen groups. But Diane's mother was not happy in their new surroundings. She had spent so many years protecting herself from trouble and railing against urban conditions that peace was strange and uncomfortable. She missed her old friends. Birds singing in the morning, as lovely as they might be, could not replace the familiar sounds of garbage cans being tossed about, neighbors fighting, stereos blasting in the middle of the night. Change—even for a better quality of life—can be difficult to deal with. Change is the unknown, whereas the usual, as dull and even painful as it sometimes can be, is at least predictable.

Almost any choice involves compromises, so it's helpful to start the process of weighing the plus and minus factors while you're still a *Pre-REtirement Planner*. At the end of this chapter there is a test you can give yourself that will help clarify your thinking on the things you really want most in a place to live, and how important they are on a comparative scale.

IMAGE AND REALITY

Packing up and taking off for some idyllic spot is one of the prevailing images of retirement, and yet when the time comes to make that crucial choice—to stay or not to stay—the majority of retirees choose not to move. According to the latest available data, about 70 percent remain in their pre-retirement homes, another 25 percent move to smaller homes in the same county or state, and only about 5 percent of all retirees move out of their own states. It is expected, however, that with increasingly better health, possibly higher incomes, and improved housing, the 5 percent figure is likely to grow somewhat in coming years.

Interestingly, staying home is exactly what the former director of the National Institute of Aging, Dr. Robert N. Butler, thinks most people should do. "The best place to retire," he says, "is the neighborhood where you spent your life. When you move from your home, you tear apart the social fabric of your life. Friends, relatives, children, and good medical facilities are far more important than blue skies and warm weather."

Obviously, of course, that is not always the case. People may need to move for reasons of health, or for a lower cost of living, or to escape a deteriorating neighborhood, or because a complete change of locale— new friends, new activities, and a new life-style—is the retirement scenario they've been working on for years, and the one that best suits their situation.

IF YOU DECIDE TO STAY . . .

There can be advantages in staying right where you are, or in the same general area:

• You know the territory; more important, you know the people— from doctors and druggists to friends and relatives to the people who can perform services reliably. In short, you're no longer a newcomer.

• You know what it costs to live in your present location, and where the best bargains are. What's more, many of your biggest expenditures— among them your house and your furniture—are taken care of.

• Conversion possibilities offer the potential of additional retirement income. An upper story of your home, a garage, or a barn could be made into a rental unit.

• If you want to stay in the same area but need a different house (smaller, easier to care for, or better located), that option is always open. As we said earlier, you know the territory.

• Perhaps most important of all, there is the elaborate social network developed over a period of years, involving family and friends.

IF YOU DECIDE TO GO . . .

Assuming that you've discovered some promising areas for relocation, here are some basic questions that need to be asked:

• Is the climate endurable the year round?

• Is the cost of living acceptable?

• Is there adequate public transportation, or is it necessary to drive everywhere?

• Are there churches or synagogues within easy distance?

• Are there opportunities for part-time jobs, volunteer work, etc.?

• How near are doctors, dentists, and hospitals? Are they about average in cost?

• Will it be fairly easy to shop?

• Does the community strike you as friendly?

• How do local and state taxes compare with those where you live now?

• Are small children welcome? Can your grandchildren visit?

• If pets are a factor in your life, are they allowed?

The chamber of commerce in the locality in which you're interested can help you with some of those questions.

NOTES ON CLIMATE

It's easy to underestimate the importance of climate. It helps to determine the clothes you wear, the fuel bills you pay, the kind of house you need, the wear and tear on your car, and much more. Above all, weather experts say, it can strongly affect the state of your mind as well as your body. Climate played a key role in Mike and Doris Williams' decision not to move to Florida when Mike retires. They love the state and the slower pace there, and they were looking forward to being near their eldest son. But Doris and Mike, after a six-month trial stay, found to their surprise that they badly missed the change of seasons. They loved the weather on vacation, but too much of it, they found, had a depressing effect on them. For that reason more than any other, they decided not to move.

Below are some tips on weather to help guide the *Pre-RE*tirement *P*lanner:

• The generally accepted ideal climate consists of a temperature of 75 degrees during the day and about 55 degrees at night; humidity about 55 percent; a smog- and dust-free atmosphere; and variable weather with sunshine predominating. Being the ideal, of course, that set of circumstances is rare to nonexistent, but knowing the parameters does give the *Pre-RE*tirement *P*lanner a standard against which to measure.

• In general, if you make a radical change in climate, allow a few months for your digestive system, sleeping habits, and general physical state to catch up fully.

• Most people need at least a month to adjust to warm climates. (There are a very few who can never adjust; that is a rare problem, but one that does occur.)

• It takes at least several months to adjust to colder climates, and both cold and dampness can aggravate arthritis and joint problems.

• High altitudes, starting at 6,000 to 7,000 feet, can require from one to six months for adjustment. And again, there are those who will never be able to adjust.

• Constant sunshine can be nearly as depressing as constant rain, and it induces lethargy in most people. A variable climate with plenty of sunny days is preferable.

• When you check local climates, look at the daily temperature and humidity *ranges,* not just at the averages.

REGIONAL DIFFERENCES IN MEDICAL COSTS

As the table on page 122 shows you, there are sharp differences between one area of the country and another in the overall cost of living. These differences can become acute in such a vital area as medical care, where the majority of retirees have to pay the cost of their own medical insurance. Below are examples of differences in costs among cities, as of 1987:

Location	Average Hospital Charge for Room and Board	Average Surgeon's Charge for Routine Appendectomy
Asheville, NC	$133.55	$ 760
Atlanta, GA	152.24	1,080
Charleston, SC	163.00	1,160
Chicago, IL	319.15	1,165
Los Angeles, CA	302.85	1,600
New York Metro.	312.28	2,100
Tampa, FL	176.35	1,125

TAX DIFFERENCES

One more key area in which you'll find major differences is state and local taxation. In general, taxes are highest in the Northeast and lowest in the North Central states. The West tends to have higher taxes than the South. And Nevada, with no inheritance or estate taxes, no state income tax, and only mild property taxes, is quite a bargain.

Some states offer personal and property tax breaks for people 65

WHAT IT COSTS TO LIVE WHERE

The table below lists comparative price indexes for selected cities against a national average index of 100. Data in the table come from the American Chamber of Commerce Researchers Association for the third quarter of 1987.*

City & State	100 All-Items Index
Birmingham, AL	99.0
Phoenix, AZ	106.3
Los Angeles County, CA	115.4
Orange County, CA	118.9
San Diego, CA	118.9
Denver, CO	102.3
Hartford, CT	119.2
Ft. Lauderdale, FL	112.9**
Miami, FL	112.4
Atlanta, GA	110.8
Indianapolis, IN	97.4
Louisville, KY	96.3
Baton Rouge, LA	98.0
Portland, ME	105.9**
Newark/Elizabeth/Jersey City, NJ	127.6**
Albuquerque, NM	104.1
New York, NY	145.8
Syracuse, NY	94.6
Charlotte, NC	100.0
Philadelphia, PA	122.0
Greenville, SC	94.9
Houston, TX	100.4

*Differences of 3 or fewer index points are not statistically significant and do not necessarily indicate even the direction of any difference in living costs.

**Did not participate. Figure shown as of third quarter of 1986.

and older; in many instances, however, there's the requirement that you must live in the state for a specified period of time (usually a year) to be eligible. Free booklets are available which list tax facts for every state.

You'll find states with no personal income taxes, and some with no general sales taxes. But remember that handy acronym TINSTAAFL, which stands for one of the great rules of our time: *There is no such thing as a free lunch.* A low tax rate usually means a low level of public services—hospitals, recreation, fire and police protection, sanitation services, and social services. It's wise to consider the trade-offs you'll be making in exchange for tax breaks.

HOW TO RATE RETIREMENT HAVENS

Now that many Sunbelt sites have become crowded and high in cost, and now, too, that congestion has brought such urban problems as air pollution and water scarcity to many areas, experts on locales for retired people have been combing the country to find new bargains. One solution is the smaller city, or rural area, in a pleasant climate. "We are seeing a back-to-the-village movement among a growing number of retirees," says one national real estate consultant. Population movement to smaller towns is occurring in California, Arizona and Florida, among other states.

You *Pre-REtirement Planners* may find the following criteria useful in establishing guidelines of your own:

• *Climate:* On most days, temperature should average 65 degrees, and humidity 55 percent.

• *Cost of living:* Retired couples should be able to live reasonably well for around $13,000 a year, and should be paying approximately 8 percent of their income for state and local taxes.

• *Housing:* There should be a variety of two-bedroom units available from $50,000.

• *Medical facilities:* Hospital and semiprivate rates should be less than $250 a day. There should be at least one doctor for every 750 people.

• *Recreation and culture:* There should be ample facilities to suit your interests.

• *Special services:* For people 65 and older, low-cost transportation and other services are desirable.

Nothing, of course, will take the place of personal inspection and firsthand study. But when you have pinned down a few likely prospects, you may find it helpful and interesting to subscribe to local newspapers for several months. They will tell you a great deal.

Also, be sure to contact the chamber of commerce in the locality you are interested in for information on housing, taxes, etc. It is a prime source of hard facts.

AN APARTMENT OR SMALLER HOUSE

If you have decided that your present home is not a satisfying solution for your retirement, you should consider the advantages and disadvantages of moving into a cooperative or condominium apartment or a smaller house. An apartment gives you the luxury of locking the door and taking off at a moment's notice. Maintenance problems are not yours; plumbing and heating difficulties belong to the superintendent. There is no lawn to mow or snow to shovel. Living in an apartment building can give you a sense of security; you simply know that someone is nearby. This could be a way of making new friends, particularly if there are public lounges and recreation centers, including a pool and tennis courts. But there are also, of course, the negatives to consider: neighbors who are inconsiderate about noise, a landlord or manager who does not provide proper services such as heat or ensure cleanliness and safe elevators, and, in the case of renters, lack of equity.

A smaller house would give you a scaled-down version of previous housing, but if you decide on a smaller house, be aware that in retirement you are likely to spend more time with your mate. You must allow for privacy and for ''territorial rights'' involving hobbies. A recent CBS retiree and his wife sold their home and bought a smaller one, and soon after, to their chagrin, realized their mistake. He needed extra space to accommodate both his ham radio and airplane-connected hobbies, and with her growing interest in painting she needed a studio.

On the plus side, a smaller house costs less to maintain and involves less upkeep and labor.

If you decide that the answer is a co-op or condominium, it is important to understand the key differences between the two. The buyer of a condominium buys not only a housing unit—the living space itself—but a share in the common areas: the land it is built on, the surrounding grounds, halls, elevators, lobby, swimming pool, etc. You usually get your own mortgage and are not responsible if other owners default.

The buyer of a co-op does not buy a unit but rather shares in a corporation, the shares of which are in proportion to the size of the unit occupied. A tenant shareholder has the right to occupy the space enclosed by the walls, floor, and ceiling of his apartment, but ownership of the walls, floors and ceiling, along with the common areas, remains with the cooperative corporation. You have to seek board approval before buying (which is not the case when buying a condo), and the financial standards set for potential cooperators can be rigorous.

You should hire a real estate lawyer before buying any type of housing. If you don't know such a specialist, the local bar association will recommend names for your choice. This is surely too important and serious a step to take without a legal representative; you should not sign even what appears to be an innocuous piece of paper or make any sort of deposit without prior consultation with a lawyer representing your— and no one else's—interests. Resist pressures to make you commit. The more pressure, the more need for caution. If the dream is worthwhile, it will bear scrutiny.

If your decision is to relocate, it is recommended that you separate the move from the actual time of retirement. There is enough stress and change in leaving one's job and colleagues without adding the pressures of selling, packing, moving, and reestablishing oneself at the same time. Be kind to yourself. Choose a time when you have become accustomed to the changes inherent in retirement daily living.

But whatever you ultimately decide—whether it is to stay where you are or to relocate—make it thoughtfully with your partner. Each of you should draw up a list of what you want in your new community, compare notes, and come to a mutual decision. Simply moving to satisfy the needs of one of you is not the sensible way to make such an important decision. Because you both have to live there, you should face all of the pros and cons realistically and together.

A PERSONAL PROFILE

Here are some of the foremost considerations in choosing a place to live that may help you clarify your and/or your spouse's desires. Check off your preference under each heading, and then rate the importance you attach to it on a scale from 1 (least) to 10. The answers should give you a fair rundown of your inclination.

PREFERENCE	IMPORTANCE (1 to 10)
1. CLIMATE	
___Warmer ___Cooler ___Same as now	___
2. REGION	
___Northeast ___Southeast ___Central ___Southwest ___West	___
3. KIND OF COMMUNITY	
___City ___Town or village ___Rural ___Vacation resort	___
4. TERRAIN	
___Mountainous ___Seashore ___Desert ___Good for gardening (wherever it is)	___
5. HOUSING	
___Mobile home ___Condo ___Own house ___Adult community or residence ___Apartment ___Other	___
6. TRANSPORTATION	
___Drive own car ___Public transportation	___

Part 3

YOUR HEALTH: A VITAL LEGACY

10

Health and Medical Care

We will start this section with some hard facts that the pre-retiree should know about medical care. In 1900, 3 million Americans—or 4 percent of the population—were over the age of 65. In 1987, 30 million Americans—or 12 percent—were 65 or older. It is estimated that by the year 2030 we will have 64 million Americans, or 22 percent of the population, over the age of 65. If 65 continues to be the mandatory retirement age in the United States, we will probably be bankrupt within the next forty years. We cannot afford to have 22 percent of our population over the age of 65 and hope to keep things the way they are at present. First of all, most of the 22 percent would be out of work and collecting Social Security—if there *is* Social Security. Chances are there won't be enough people working to pay for it. We also won't be able to pay for Medicare. What is frightening economically is that not only are more people going to reach age 65, but the fastest-growing segment of the American population is actually *85 and above*. So by the year 2030, when we have 64 million people over the age of 65, 30 million are going to be over 75, and 12 million over 85.

If you're a health economist you have to ask yourself a simple but vital question: is 65 what it was twenty years ago, and is it now what it will be twenty years hence? Today in geriatrics we call 65 to 75 young, and the 75-to-85 range middle age. Age 65 as a retirement age was passed down to us from Otto von Bismarck's Germany. When Bismarck was unifying the German state he promised pensions and free medical care at retirement to those who worked for the central government. Although retirement age was 65, the life expectancy in Germany at that time was about 50; thus Bismarck wasn't giving much away.

But what is the logic in using 65 as the retirement age today? Nothing happens to us at 65. The government, given the problems it will be facing with a country full of old people, has begun to pass legislation raising the mandatory retirement age, and many states are beginning to do away with mandatory retirement. The government no longer wants people to retire; the consequences could be economically ruinous. It would much prefer that you keep working and paying taxes until you're 120, if you're able.

The government is also beginning to ask why people should begin collecting Social Security benefits at 65. There is talk of raising the age to 67, even 70. Health economists are beginning to ask why Social Security should be paid to anyone on a pension, and others are asking a more radical question: why should we pay Social Security *at all?* The answer to both questions is that the government entered into a contract with us in which we give money while we work and will get money on retirement. But governments are not bound to keep their promises when they feel the commonwealth is at stake.

Next, there is the problem of health costs, which have gotten seriously out of hand. In 1984, the United States spent about $400 billion on health, or 11 percent of the gross national product. Of this, about half the money was coming from the federal government, much of it in the form of Medicare and Medicaid. Feeling the pinch, the government set out to determine where the money was being spent and where cutbacks could be effected.

The largest amount is spent on hospital care: almost 50 percent goes to acute-care hospitals. The government has created the DRG (disease-related grouping) system as a means of limiting this staggering expense. First of all, you cannot go into the hospital to get tests; you can only use the hospital to get treatment that can't be done elsewhere. When you go into a hospital—which in New York City costs about $800 a day—the doctor makes a diagnosis, and depending on that diagnosis, you have only so many days in the hospital that Medicare will pay for.

Say, for example, that you have pneumonia and the DRG for pneumonia is seven days. Under DRG, the hospital gets paid for seven days. If you stay longer, the hospital assumes the loss, whereas if you stay for a shorter period, the hospital makes the profit. So if you're a hospital administrator the dream is to have rapid patient turnover. The ideal patient is one who comes in with a long DRG and dies in five minutes.

This year, the *New York Times* listed hospitals where a more than average percentage of elderly patients were dying, many of them soon after admittance. It wasn't that those hospitals were necessarily poorly run: they were simply choosing terminal cases in order to get substantial DRGs which would make them a greater profit. If there are three patients, and one is going to die any second, one will get better within a week, and the third is going to be a long and complicated case, you might take one of the first two but send the third one packing. Let some other institution worry about him; he's a real money-loser.

The DRG system—inefficient and unfair in many ways—may not even be saving money. Bureaucracies have had to be set up in each hospital; there is a huge bureaucracy in Washington. There are bureaucracies overseeing the regulatory bureaucracies—and all of them tend to eat up any of the cost savings the DRG system might have created.

When you check into a hospital the first question you are asked is how you're going to pay. The second question is how you're going to get home. If you're lucky, someone might ask you about the state of your health. If you're on Medicare you must have a prearranged plan so that you don't overstay the stipulated period. You're worried, you're frightened, you're going into the hospital and signing papers agreeing to pay anything Medicare doesn't pay. Secondly, sick or well, you're promising to leave whenever your time runs out, even if you leave on a stretcher. In medical parlance that's known as getting out quicker and sicker.

Physicians' services take a big slice of the medical pie. To give you an idea of costs, the average surgeon in New York City is charging $2,000 per hour of operating time. Because operations run from two to five hours, surgeons make between $4,000 and $10,000 per operation. This sounds like more money than it actually is, however. In New York a surgeon may spend $100,000 a year or more on malpractice insurance, and the costs of running and renting an office will add an additional $100,000 annually. With an overhead of $200,000 a year, it's no wonder that surgeons' costs are so high.

The government is making an effort to cut back on the enormous costs of medical care. In some states—for example, Massachusetts—doctors have to accept Medicare assignments, and they have to accept what Medicare pays. In Massachusetts, Medicare pays about $25 a visit. In Boston, where the physician spends $40 an hour on average to rent an office, it's very hard to see a patient for whose visit he will be paid $25. And of course besides the $40 for office space, he's paying for malpractice insurance, medical supplies, and secretarial help. As a result, doctors live in dread of seeing Medicare patients. They tend to be sicker than other patients and to take more time, and the doctor can charge only whatever the government has decided the patient must pay. Therefore in states like Massachusetts the crisis grows as more and more doctors refuse to see Medicare patients.

The government has also decided to try to foster the HMOs, or health maintenance organizations. Some HMOs are very good indeed. But occasionally unscrupulous HMOs take control of the patients' payments and disappear with the money. You must make certain before signing with an HMO plan that it will cover you out of state or out of the country, if you're traveling. Unfortunately, some do not.

There is another catch in some of the new HMOs. Say you are suddenly in great pain from an infected gall bladder and you must have it removed. You go to see your doctor and he's too swamped to schedule you for an operation. Your doctor agrees that you definitely need the operation—so what does he do? He schedules you for surgery three or six months from today. Your answer is that you can't wait that long. The HMO explains that their surgeon is very busy and that if you want surgery sooner you can always go to another surgeon at another hospital. You next see a surgeon who is not connected with your HMO and discover that your health plan will pay for very little—if any—of your care outside of the HMO restrictions. The HMO is happy because you've saved it money. This kind of problem is inherent in the HMO structure. After all, you've already paid for your care, but if an HMO is going to make a profit the last thing it needs is for you to come in demanding an operation. Operations are expensive. Also, doctors' incentives in HMOs are often linked to their keeping down costs. What the HMO wants is healthy patients—patients who pay for the services and then never have to use them, and who never have to take expensive tests.

We are not suggesting that all HMOs operate this way, or even that the concept of the HMO is inherently bad. However, we are pointing out that today many HMOs and other health plans are run for profit by businessmen, and to some your health is much less important than the profit you represent. When buying a health insurance plan—as when buying a car—you *Pre-REtirement Planners* must be educated consumers.

You should know that Medicare does not pay for many medications outside of a hospital. It does pay for certain medical appliances, if the physician can justify that the patient needs them for a medical reason. Unfortunately, it is sometimes the way a form is filled out rather than the patient's needs that determines what will be obtained.

Nursing home and home care in the United States costs somewhere around $100 million each year. In New York City, a nursing home costs up to $200 per day, and again, Medicare pays for very little of this, if any. Disregard what the booklets say; it is rare for Medicare to pay for any nursing home expenses, which means that the patient has to pay for the service out of his own pocket until such time as he is ''medically impoverished,'' to use a euphemism. The definition of ''impoverished'' varies a little from state to state, but it means that you have less than $5,000 in savings. At that point you are eligible for Medicaid, the government plan for the indigent. Medicaid will pay for all care for the rest of the patient's life. However, Medicaid tends to pay at very low reimbursement rates, and it's not easy to find an institution or doctor that will take Medicaid patients.

What does all this mean for you *Pre-REtirement Planners*? It means that our present health care system is stacked against the elderly, the poor, and the sick, who are seen as a drain on the economy of the United States. There is talk now of rationing health care. For example, some health economists are saying that as a nation we should not have to pay for such things as cancer treatments, heart operations, and dialysis in people over the age of 65.

For the *Pre-REtirement Planner* who has prepared carefully for the twenty-five years of retirement ahead, the current crisis in health care may well be of major concern—especially if he or she is even moderately wealthy. Health care is expensive, and from day to day the government is changing its mind as to how much it's willing to pay for. Private insurance companies are not covering the gap between Medicare and your pocket. The entire area of health economics is in a state of flux, and it is virtually impossible for an individual to buy sufficient insurance to protect himself. You must belong to a group and hope that the company you work for will extend its insurance coverage to you when you retire and will continue to cover your surviving spouse if you should die first.

Now that we have explored the health economics picture, it is clear that if you get sick all of your financial planning can go out the window. Most financial projections presume that you will be relatively healthy. We therefore must turn to health and the vital question of how—and for how long—you can remain healthy. In the following chapters we will discuss what aging means and its physical and mental effects, what diseases are likely to incapacitate us and what ones will kill us, and the positive steps you *Pre-REtirement Planners* can take to remain healthy into extreme old age.

11

Our Biological Clock

When we talk about aging and health it is important to remember that aging is a biological phenomenon. It occurs in all animals except certain species of reptiles and fish. Aging can be defined as a gradual decline in all body functions, and the process of growing old is extremely difficult to study in people. The ideal experiment would be to take children at birth, study them throughout their lives, and see what factors lead to good and to faulty aging. Because such a study would take nearly a century to do successfully, researchers have turned instead to the rat model as the best alternative to studying humans. Now what do we know about rats? On the average, they live to the age of nine months. Usually they either contract a fatal infectious disease or get run over by a car, eaten by a cat, or caught in a rat trap.

In order for rats to extend their life expectancy beyond nine months there are four simple steps to take. The rat must be removed from its natural environment, put into a laboratory, cleaned up so that it doesn't get rat infectious diseases, and protected from cars, cats, and traps—and then rats will live an average of eighteen months, at which time they will die of heart or kidney disease, cancer, or a form of arthritis very similar to what will kill humans.

In order for rats to live still longer, their calories must be cut by one-third. Now, instead of a fat, middle-aged, eighteen-month-old rat, you have a slimmer rat that will live slightly over two years on the average. While the calories are being cut, the fat in the rat's diet must be reduced; as a result, fewer rats get cancer. When protein in the diet is limited, many fewer rats are victims of heart and kidney disease and arthritis.

To add still more time to their life expectancy, rats must be put in a cage with other rats. They need friends. Rats, like humans, are social animals. They like their rat society. When they are allowed to socialize, they add more months to their lives.

The fourth step in lengthening their longevity is to give them exercise—exercise they enjoy. Rats hate to swim. Psychologists have measured the effect on them and it is decidedly negative—so much so that swimming will actually *shorten* their life expectancy. Rats, however, love mazes. Give them a maze to run around in and food at the end of it and their day is made. Proper exercise, then, adds a number of months more to their lives.

Finally, for the male rat (this is not true for the female, a fact which we will discuss in greater detail later), an active sex life adds still more months to its life span.

By following these five steps—paying attention to the environment, food, exercise, sociability, and sexuality—we can now keep rats alive an average of three and a half to four years. We have quadrupled an animal species' life expectancy, not by treating rats' diseases or giving them antibiotics or any form of medication but simply by improving their life-style. Granted, they will still die of heart and kidney disease, cancer, and arthritis, but one to two years later. In other words, the development of these illnesses has been postponed.

But what does this have to do with people? The answer is that there is a close correlation between the needs of rats and the needs of people. Environment, nutrition, sociability, exercise, and sexuality are among the five priority areas of research of the National Institute of Aging of the National Institutes of Health.

What do we know of human beings in relation to aging? The first clue can be found in the Bible. Moses came down from Mt. Sinai when he was 80 years old and at the height of his career. The Bible goes on to tell us something very important: when Moses died at the age of 120 he wasn't blind, nor was his physical and mental force abated. Nor, from the available evidence, was he either sick or weak.

Then why did he die? The general consensus in modern medicine is that the human life span, with all disease eradicated and under optimum conditions, could be extended out to Moses's 120 years. Just as every animal species seems to have a definite longevity, 120 years would appear to be the biological clock that is set in us. Beyond that point, it seems, we cannot go.

The Bible tells us that Moses was still strong at 120. We're finding out now that the aging process need not be as terrible as it was thought to be in previous generations. Most of the negative aspects of aging actually have nothing to do with the *process* of aging but are connected with disease. That is an important distinction to make, because disease can be fought, whereas natural process is to a great extent inevitable. This is another way of saying that the enemy is disease, not the biological process of aging.

The oldest human being whose age we can verify (the birth was registered by the state) was a Japanese male who turned 120 in 1985. He was in excellent condition, and, at that great age, appeared on U.S. television with his children, grandchildren, and great- and great-great-grandchildren. Two months later he contracted pneumonia and died. This man, it would seem, had reached the final tick of our biological clock.

In the 1960s a segment of American youth extolled the virtues of nature; these children of privilege were convinced that modern industrial society was killing us and that in order to survive we had better return to the land where life was much healthier. Looking at this argument in terms of a life-expectancy curve, we have to return to the rats. Are we like them in that we do better in a protected environment? The answer is a resounding yes. The average life expectancy of your typical cave man was 15 years; most people in those days died before 30 and almost no one reached 50. You were old by the time you were 20. The natural state, then, does not seem conducive to good health and a long life.

In Mexico, in 1930, the average life expectancy was 25 years. In 1900, an American's average life expectancy was 55; in 1945 it had risen to 62, and now the average life expectancy is 78. What happened in 1945 that made such a dramatic difference? Put simply, we entered the antibiotic era. First there was sulfa, and then, much more significant in its impact, penicillin. These drugs have added almost two decades to the lives of Americans.

Average life expectancy, by the way, does not mean that at age 65 you have 13 years left to live. It means that you're born at a certain point in time with all types of mortality taken into account. By the time you reach 65, you actually have a life expectancy (on the average for age 65) of another 20 years. When you reach 75, you still have another 12 years. When you get to 85, you have on an average another 7 or 8 years. In other words, the older you get the longer, on an average, you're going to live.

It should be pointed out, however, that while life expectancy in the United States has grown steadily longer and is now 78, we rank only about fifteenth in the world. Japan is number one, followed by Sweden, Norway, and Denmark. Also ahead of us are the other northern European—and most of the Mediterranean—countries. Interestingly, the Japanese in Japan outlive Japanese-Americans, and that is true of those from other countries as well, which would suggest that healthier diets exist outside the United States—a point we will return to later.

In countries like Haiti, Upper Volta, Chad, and Ethiopia, life expectancies are still less than 30 years, a further resounding vote against the primitive—or ''natural''—cultural utopia. While it is clear that modern industrial society is far from perfect, statistics show that you will live much longer in our developed world than in an undeveloped nation.

Taking a closer look at the statistical breakdown for longevity, you will notice first of all that there is a significant difference between men and women, just as there is between the black and white population of the United States. It is a commonly held belief that women outlive men because they suffer less stress. It isn't true. The principal reason has to do with the hormonal differences between the sexes. Men begin to get hardening of the arteries as soon as they go through puberty. Women, however, are protected against atherosclerosis until they reach menopause. Thus the average woman, unless she has diabetes or abnormally high blood pressure or smokes cigarettes, has arteries at age 50 equal to those of a boy of 12. Heart attacks and strokes are rare in women before menopause, while they are all too common in men in their 30s, 40s, and 50s.

Although both sexes make both male and female hormones, men produce predominantly the male hormone testosterone, and women the female hormones estrogen and progesterone. There is now evidence that the female hormones protect the arteries from atherosclerosis. Only after menopause, when the woman makes far less of these hormones, does she begin to get hardening of the arteries.

There is also a significant difference in longevity between blacks and whites in this country. One of the major reasons for this is high blood pressure. Young black men especially are susceptible to the effects of hypertension. However, if a black person makes it to 65, he or she is much more likely than a Caucasian to live to 100. Medical science has no idea why the majority of centenarians in America are black; it is a subject of ongoing research.

In the past fifteen years the most important contribution to increased life expectancy in the United States was the reduction of highway speed limits to 55 and the mandatory requirement that seat belts be put into automobiles. Most fatal accidents happen to our under-25 population, particularly males. Thus when you reduce that mortality the numbers for longevity are greatly affected. Statistically, if you always drive without speeding and use your seat belt at all times, you are increasing your life expectancy on the average of one and a half years.

The human life span is finite, but it does seem to reach out to 120 years. Most people at today's normal retirement age of 65, if they are now healthy, should have on the average another 20 years of life ahead of them. The goal of modern medicine is to allow all people to live between 80 and 100 years. By taking good care of ourselves we should be able to achieve that goal.

Many people say that they would rather not live into old age because aging does terrible things to the body and mind. This shows an ignorance of the facts of aging's *process*. Let us now turn to an examination of what aging really does to us.

12

Aging and Disease

From a biological standpoint, we are at our best the moment the egg and sperm come together and create us. That is when we grow the fastest, doubling to become two cells. We have the greatest potential: everything is going to grow. At age 20 we tend to be at our physical prime, and from that point on we decline; by 30 we can all notice a slight physical deterioration. Between 30 and 60 we lose roughly half of our lung function, even if we breathe good air and don't smoke. Also between 30 and 60 we lose half of our muscle function, unless we exercise vigorously, in which case we lose about one-quarter. Other functions go down as well. The heart goes down only about 25 percent between 35 and 70; the brain, the best-protected organ we have, goes down only 10 percent between 40 and 80.

This may all sound terrible to anyone who is aging—body functions diminishing, everything going downhill—but luckily we were born with two to seven times as much of everything as we need. That's our reserve. So even if we lose 50 percent of this and 30 percent of that, we still have an ample supply of everything—that is, unless we are under tremendous stress.

The worst form of stress is disease. When we get sick we depend upon our reserve to make us better. It is also the body's reserve response that gives us the typical signs and symptoms of an illness. As we get older, therefore, the typical signs of an illness are absent, changed, or delayed—for example, the classic signs and symptoms of a heart attack, including squeezing pain in the front center to left part of the chest, sweating, nausea, shortness of breath, and a tremendous sensation of fear; 75 percent of older people will not have these symptoms. In some the only sign will be shortness of breath; others will become mentally confused; and in still others the heart attack will be totally silent. It is only when that person goes for an electrocardiogram that the heart damage is discovered.

Pneumococcal pneumonia provides another example of how differently the elderly respond to serious illness. A study at the NYU-Bellevue Medical Center showed that almost 40 percent of the older people admitted with the condition did not have fever. In young people with this type of pneumonia, 100 percent had fever on admission. The older you get the longer it takes to mount a fever. This means that a serious physical problem in the elderly can be masked, and for that reason those of retirement age and older should have a doctor who knows them very well and will be able to tell when they are sick. The physician should listen carefully and not attribute to age subtle changes in the degree of physical well-being.

As we grow older, the effects of drugs are usually more pronounced and adverse reactions are more likely. Take medications only under the direction of a physician. Over-the-counter drugs—even vitamin pills and food supplements—can be dangerous. Again, it's best to consult with your physician before taking anything.

In older people, medications and various illnesses commonly cause mental confusion, which is not part of normal aging and should never be accepted as such. If someone's mind is not working normally, it is essential to see a doctor. When an elderly person complains of a host of physical symptoms, remember that this could be a psychological problem. Patients who are depressed often complain of weakness, tiredness, loss of appetite, weight loss, constipation, and generalized aches and pains.

It used to be said that the United States was a depressing country in which to age because we were such a youth-oriented society. The situation has changed in recent years. More and more of us are getting older. Many of our media stars are in their 50s, 60s, and above. Most of us, it seems, find most attractive that which resembles us. Therefore, as the nation ages we find comfort rather than sadness in the fact of growing older, and perhaps even an element of glamour in the attributes that go with greater age—a more highly developed intelligence and keener judgment. Advertisers have discovered that this increasingly larger group of older people is a considerable consumer force. Retirees are buying more all the time, and they're being catered to. They are developing power in the marketplace, and a voice. It may not be mere coincidence that our national leader is a man in his mid-70s.

What are the physical changes in a person the age of Ronald Reagan? The first thing you notice is that the ears and nose are taking up more space on the face. The reason is that cartilage keeps growing over a longer period of time than bones do. Our weight, on the other hand, tends to decrease as we age, because we're losing muscle and bone; if your weight does not decrease it means that you're substituting fat for muscle and bone. The bone loss particularly affects women and can lead to osteoporosis. With age, we also grow shorter—again, this happens to women more than men because of osteoporosis, which causes the vertebrae to collapse. Lung and kidney efficiency in a person Reagan's age are down by 50 percent. Hearing is down, especially the high tones. Eyes go down, starting in the early 40s, and usually by 45 most people will need bifocals or reading glasses.

The thymus gland, the master gland of immunity, which is located in the chest on top of the heart, also loses function as we age, and as a result we become increasingly susceptible to various infectious diseases, and to cancer. It is part of the immune system that is involved with the so-called T-cell (thymus-derived) immunity, the system that is broken down by the viral disease AIDS. The changes that afflict AIDS patients are similar to those that occur in the normal aging process; young men are now prey to diseases that previously were seen only in very old men—principally Kaposi's sarcoma and pneumocystis pneumonia. Because failure of the immune system is one of the major problems of aging, all that is now being discovered about AIDS will prove of enormous benefit to our growing over-65 population.

How do living arrangements affect longevity? Fifty-one percent of retired people are living with their spouses (a percentage that would be higher if we could find a way to keep men alive longer, or if women would marry younger men). Twenty-seven percent, for the most part women, are living alone. Men tend to fare poorly on their own; in some studies as many as 50 percent of males died within one year after the death of the spouse unless they had remarried. It has been found that when a man's wife dies the man suddenly has a breakdown of his immune system, just as if he had caught AIDS. The life expectancy of women, however, is not appreciably affected by the loss of their husbands, a fact that medical science cannot as yet account for.

THE KILLER DISEASES

The leading cause of death in the United States is cardiovascular disease. Strokes have fallen from second to third place—and in fact both heart attacks and strokes are on the decrease, not only in the United States but throughout the world. Cancer has risen to second place and continues on the rise. Number four is influenza. The key challenge in medical science is to find ways to prevent—or retard—these diseases in order to increase life expectancy.

Age is the biggest risk factor in heart attacks and strokes, and, as discussed earlier, a man is at particular risk of encountering vascular problems in his 40s and 50s because his arteries begin to harden at puberty. Your family history also defines your risk of getting a heart attack or stroke. If you are 60 years old and both of your parents died of either disease before the age of 65, you have about a 10 percent chance of having a heart attack or stroke in the next five years. If you add high blood pressure, your chances are 20 percent. Add diabetes and your chances rise to 40 percent. If you also have high cholesterol you're in the 80 percent bracket. Worst of all, if you're a cigarette smoker you are virtually guaranteed to have a heart attack or a stroke by your 65th birthday.

With cancer, the biggest risk is also age. Despite what you might read, you are more likely to develop cancer the older you get. Even cancers we associate with youth are more common in the elderly. For example, the so-called childhood leukemia is three times more common in people over age 65 than in children. Cigarette smoking and environmental carcinogens are major contributors in developing cancer, and heredity plays a major role in certain forms of the disease.

The biggest cancer killer attacks the lungs, and 70 percent of cases are caused by cigarette smoking and environmental carcinogens. Unfortunately, there is no reliable screening test to detect lung cancer. A chest X-ray may pick it up, but that type of cancer grows so quickly that as a preventive measure you would have to have a chest X-ray every week, and if you didn't have cancer of the lung the weekly chest X-rays would surely give it to you. The only reliable safeguard is to stop smoking.

The second most prevalent cancer affects the colon, and it can be inherited and is also partially related to the American diet, which is low in complex carbohydrates. In Japan, where the diet is high in complex carbohydrates, cancer of the colon is rare. Everyone—particularly those of retirement age—should have a yearly rectal examination. Almost half of all colon cancer may be within reach of the examining finger. You also should have your stools checked for blood; those cancers that are not felt on rectal examination usually leak small amounts of blood into the stool.

One of every eleven American women will die of breast cancer, even though it is among the most curable of all cancers. The operation is relatively simple, and the older you are when you get breast cancer the more likely it is that surgery will cure you. It is important that a woman do a self-examination of her breasts once a month and see a doctor twice a year. Young women with a family history of breast cancer should also have a mammogram once a year. All women over the age of 65 should have annual mammography.

Cancer of the prostate in men is extremely common. This gland may be felt on rectal examination, and, as in the case of colon cancer, the disease often can be detected by that simple method.

Cancer of the uterus and ovaries in women can be picked up through a thorough pelvic examination. It is not to be confused with cancer of the cervix, a young woman's disease that is detected by means of a Pap smear. Every woman needs a pelvic examination once a year; if there are any abnormalities, other tests are essential.

Cancers of the urinary tract, bladder, and kidneys are also very common. Some of these are caused by pollutants in our environment which are taken into our body in food, water, and air and excreted through the urine. Since they pass through the kidneys and bladder, they act as carcinogens at those sites. To screen for these cancers, the urine must be checked periodically for blood.

Cancers of the lymphatic system (lymphoma) and of the blood (leukemia) are also fairly common, and the chances of getting one or the other increase the older we get. Acute lymphoblastic leukemia is 70 percent curable in children but virtually incurable in the elderly. On the other hand, chronic lymphocytic leukemia is a common ailment among the elderly and does not exist in children. Many older people who develop this form of cancer will live for another ten to twenty years without any symptoms.

Influenza and pneumonia are the fourth leading cause of death in the United States. It is recommended that anyone with a chronic disease, and *all* people over the age of 65, have a flu shot once a year. There is also an immunization against twenty-three varieties of pneumococcal pneumonia. It is a once-in-a-lifetime shot that seems to provide lifetime immunity.

Heart disease, cancer, strokes, and infections are the major causes of death in our retired population. Now we will turn to the major causes of incapacity in the retirement years: depression, incontinence, amputations, hip fractures, and senility.

CAUSES OF INCAPACITY

More common than is generally recognized, depression affects approximately 20 percent of all people over the age of 65. There are basically two types of depression—endogenous (coming from within), and exogenous (coming from without). Endogenous depression, which has a biological basis and can be inherited, is caused by a change in the chemistry of the brain, and the older you are the more likely it is this change will lead to depression. Psychiatrists are very successful in treating endogenous depression, because with proper medication the patient almost always gets better. Unfortunately, exogenous depression is much more difficult to cure or control. Because its roots are psychological and social rather than in the patient's chemical makeup, there is no specific drug cure. The patient may need extensive therapy, or perhaps a change in his or her social situation.

Both types of depression are common at the time of retirement, and one can often predict those who will become depressed during that period of great stress. First of all, if someone has a history of recurrent depression, retirement may trigger it. Second, certain psychological types are prone to depression when they retire. If you are the kind of person who wakes up every Monday morning feeling wonderful, jumps out of bed and can hardly wait to get to the office, and keeps on feeling wonderful until Friday afternoon, when you begin to suffer a sinking sensation at the prospect of a weekend away from the office, then retirement may well be a disaster for you. On the other hand, if Friday afternoon brings bliss, and you hate getting out of bed Monday morning, then you should probably have retired twenty years ago.

Urinary incontinence is very common in the elderly and is curable in only about 20 percent of cases. However, it is virtually always manageable. There are many new absorbent undergarments on the market that do not show underneath clothing and allow the person to handle the problem in a discreet and sanitary manner. Urinary incontinence should not hamper one from living a normal life.

Leg amputations occur mainly in people with diabetes. Now that we have better methods for controlling diabetes, we will see fewer amputations in the future.

Those patients with osteoporosis and severe osteoarthritis are susceptible to hip fractures and the malfunctioning of the spine and knees. Osteoporosis, an inherited disease, can be at least partially prevented with careful attention to one's hormones, exercise, and diet. Geriatric research has shown that it is far safer to undergo a hip operation before you are crippled than after, and that new surgical techniques of total hip and knee replacements can prevent the most crippling effects of osteoarthritis. Also new methods of rehabilitation are now restoring many people to full activity.

Senility is perhaps the number-one worry of the aging and their relatives, and it is the leading reason why the elderly go into nursing homes. But is senility an inevitable part of aging? The answer is no—there is nothing normal about senility at any age. Often when older people complain about losing their memory they are worrying needlessly: the brain is simply changing its way of functioning.

The brain is composed of two halves, the left and the right, which are connected by the corpus collosum. The left brain is the intellect and deals with mathematics, logic, and language. If someone asks you for the sum of two and two and you answer four, your left brain hemisphere is being addressed and it's the left side that answers. The right hemisphere is the dreamer: it handles music, art, and spatial relations. Instead of talking, the right brain thinks in pictures. If you are told to close your eyes and imagine you're in Hawaii and the sun is shining and the palm trees are swaying in the breeze above and in the background you hear music, you are being asked to use your right brain.

Then comes the crossover, what people think of as "memory." When someone asks you what you're thinking about, the right brain has to send a message across to the left brain in order for the left brain to answer: "Hawaii." In aging, the left brain actually improves about 10 percent. In other words, we become more intelligent, more adept at using language. At the same time, however, the right brain diminishes by about 20 percent, and we are left with less imagination, less sense of spatial relations, and less overall creative ability. The result is what we come to fear as memory loss.

One day you're walking along the street and see an old acquaintance; you can't remember her name. You know who she is, you know a great deal about her, but her name eludes you. An hour later you say, "Oh my God, how could I have forgotten that her name's Irene? I must be slipping." The fact is, you are not slipping, nor did you forget. When you saw her, the memory came up in your brain's right hemisphere, and then the right side had to send the message to the left side—but the computer was down temporarily. The disk was overloaded. So you had to wait until the computer was up once more and sent the message "Irene!" Those suffering from true senility or dementia not only would not remember the name or recognize the person but wouldn't even remember an hour later that they'd seen a person they couldn't identify.

Retirees should realize that they are more intelligent now than ever before. Retirement might be the perfect opportunity to use that additional 10 percent left-brain power by returning to school or starting your own business. Doris Williams, for example, feels more confident of her abilities than she did in her 30s and 40s—she believes she is more logical and calmer in crises and has a better business head. She is more likely today than ever before to make a success in the collectibles market. The retiree might have to work harder than when he or she was young, but the understanding will be deeper. The extra effort should be worth the results.

Dementia is one of the more common problems we face as we age.

Approximately 10 percent of all people over the age of 65, 20 percent of people over 75, and 30 percent over 85 suffer from loss of memory, personality, judgment, orientation, and intelligence—the brain's principal functions. Dementis is *not* a normal slowing up of memory but rather a group of illnesses about 20 percent of which are curable. Curable dementias can result from many illnesses, including vitamin B_{12} deficiency; underactive or overactive thyroid; brain tumors; low or high blood pressure; abnormal salt concentrations in the blood; heart, lung, kidney, or liver disease; too many medications and/or the wrong ones; and depression.

For those with incurable dementia—the remaining 80 percent—the majority are victims of Alzheimer's disease. In the past ten years medical science has clearly defined what this illness is and we now have some good clues to what causes it. At this time, unfortunately, there is no effective treatment for Alzheimer's disease, nor any preventive measures. Other incurable forms of dementia are also found after strokes and in some patients with Parkinson's disease.

It should be stressed that a sudden confusion is never a symptom of Alzheimer's or any other dementia; by definition, sudden confusion is a delirium which always has a physical basis and can be caused by improper medications. So don't attribute the sudden confusion to age; instead, find out what's wrong and cure it. With an improvement in the patient's physical condition, the confusion will clear up.

We will now move on to a discussion of how we can stay healthy and retard the onset of old age. As we will see, like the rat we need proper exercise, a healthy diet, good sex and loving companionship.

13

Exercise, Medicine, Sex, and Nutrition

EXERCISE

Many people—particularly Americans—believe that the more exercise you do the more benefit you'll derive from it, which happens not to be true. The maximal benefit comes from expending 1,500 to 2,500 calories a week on exercise. If you lead an extremely sedentary life—sitting at a desk most of the day, lying down a great deal, walking only to go to the bathroom or to the kitchen for a meal—you will expend one calorie per minute. This is the amount of energy that your body uses up. Each minute of brisk walking is worth six calories, bicycling nine calories, swimming ten calories, and jogging fifteen to twenty calories. However, jogging is not recommended for anyone who decides to take it up at the age of 40 or over. It puts serious stress on ankles, feet, knees, and hips (often problem areas as we grow older), and there is also the risk of sudden death.

The best exercise will increase your heart rate and make you breathe a little more heavily. Walking, bicycling, swimming, and tennis are the ideal forms of exercise for the retiree (in their early 50s, Mike and Doris Williams began the habit of taking long walks on weekends, partly to help control their weight but also to enjoy the beauty of the surrounding countryside). Moderate exercise is the right exercise. An hour of tennis is fine. But two hours of singles under a hot noonday sun can be dangerous. Always check with your doctor before undertaking an exercise program and find out what you as an individual can safely tolerate. *And do not smoke!* Sucking smoke into your lungs violates all principles of good health and robs you of the hard-earned benefits of exercise.

CALORIC EXPENDITURE FOR DIFFERENT EXERCISES

Type of Activity	Calories Expended per Minute
Standing	2
Slow walking	3
Golf	3
Brisk walking	6
Dancing	6
Gardening	6
Tennis	7
Bicycling	9
Swimming	10
Walking uphill carrying bundles	10
Jogging and running	15–20

MEDICINE

As we grow older the likelihood of having to take some type of medication increases. There are medications for heart disease, infections, and cancer that have added years to the average life expectancy of Americans. For example, the antihypertensives, which control blood pressure, have been a major medical advance; and it's worth noting that had they existed in 1945, President Franklin Delano Roosevelt's blood pressure could have been kept under control and he might possibly have lived out his fourth term.

Medicines, however, are a two-edged sword and have potentially dangerous side effects, especially in the elderly. As a general rule a drug will stay in the body of a 70-year-old twice as long as in that of a 35-year-old, and the chances for a bad reaction increase. As you grow older you must be careful to take medication only under a doctor's guidance. Remember that over-the-counter medicines are indeed medicines, often extremely potent, and can cause side effects. Always tell your doctor exactly what you are taking.

Medications also may interfere with each other and with food. Let's assume, for example, you are suffering from bronchitis and your doctor prescribes tetracycline, which must be taken on an empty stomach. If you take this antibiotic with food, or with minerals (such as exist in vitamin pills), or with an antacid, or even with milk, it will not get into your bloodstream and will do nothing to cure your bronchitis. It is important to question both your doctor and pharmacist about exactly when a medication should be taken, with what type of liquid, and what the potential side effects may be.

Also, one drug can increase the effect of another drug. If you are taking warfarin (coumarin) to thin out your blood, and you take an aspirin, you could bleed to death—and you should know that more than a hundred over-the-counter medications contain aspirin. If you are taking tolbutamide (Orinase) and you drink alcohol, you could go into hypoglycemic coma.

Some drugs, on the other hand, decrease the effects of other drugs. With certain medications to lower your blood pressure, there are over-the-counter cold medicines that inactivate the antihypertensive. The cold medicines can cause certain patients suffering from high blood pressure to have a stroke, and the risk of this happening is clearly spelled out on the labels. *It is important to read the labels on all medications.*

Outdated medications may be useless or even lethal. For example, tetracycline when outdated can cause fatal kidney damage. Always check the expiration dates on labels; they are there to warn us and their instructions should be followed to the letter. If you are instructed to keep a drug in a cool, dry place, don't put it in the bathroom medicine cabinet. Bathrooms are warm and damp.

Finally, we should be wary of medications, whether outdated or not. Americans—and especially the elderly among us—tend to believe that a magic pill exists to cure whatever ails us. Without question there *are* powerful and wonderful medications, more all the time, but it is far better and easier to prevent an illness than to cure one. If we adopt a healthy life-style, don't smoke, execise steadily and intelligently, stay active and busy, monitor our diet, make sure our environment is safe, and enjoy a continuing sexual life, we will be moving in the direction of a long and healthy life in retirement.

SEX

Let us look first at the normal sexual response, how it is dependent upon hormones, and how it changes with normal aging. All of our lives both sexes make both male and female hormones. At puberty, depending on our sex, we start making much more of the male hormone (testosterone) or the female hormones (estrogen and progesterone), even though both sexes always make both types. A man at puberty—age 13—begins to make increasing amounts of testosterone, and the peak of production is reached at age 19. After that there is a slow and slight decline over the rest of the man's life, and yet at age 90 a man's testosterone level is still 90 percent of what it was at 19.

It is the high amount of testosterone in the male at the time of adulthood that drives the sexual response, and that response can be divided into four stages: excitement, plateau, orgasm, and the refractory period. During the excitement phase the man becomes interested in sexual activity and obtains an erection. The plateau takes place between the beginning of sexual intercourse and the orgasm, and the orgasm is when the man ejaculates. The refractory period is the time between orgasm and the rebirth of sexual arousal.

With age—and due to a combination of blood-vessel and brain changes rather than to loss of testosterone—it becomes increasingly difficult to get a full erection. That is part of normal aging. The plateau period increases because it takes longer to have an orgasm, the orgasm decreases in intensity, and there is less ejaculate. The refractory period also increases. In the case of a 90-year-old man the refractory period can be weeks, or even months, whereas in a 19-year-old it may be all of 30 seconds.

As women go through puberty they begin to make predominantly the female hormones estrogen and progesterone, although they still make some testosterone. Unlike men, they reach their hormonal peak at approximately age 35. After that a woman's female hormones slowly begin to decrease until she goes through menopause, at which time her hormonal level drops abruptly. It is because of this drop that women are no longer able to have babies. They now become susceptible to hot flashes, to hardening of the arteries and osteoporosis. The vaginal area and the urethra begin to dry out, also due to a decrease in estrogen.

The four stages of sexual response in women are similar to the stages in men. In the excitement stage the vagina is lubricated, and that is dependent on estrogen; next comes the plateau period, then the orgasm, and then the refractory period, which in women is very short. With aging it becomes harder for a woman to lubricate her vagina because of insufficient estrogen, although that can be cured by taking some estrogen or using an estrogen cream. The plateau period increases the same as the man's, and the orgasm also decreases in intensity. The refractory period goes up from something like half a second to a second, but is of no physical consequence in the female.

More men than women complain to doctors about sexual dysfunction. First of all, men may be trying too hard; obviously most things take more time and patience at 80 than they did at 18. Disease can cause sexual dysfunction, particularly in the man. Even with nothing more serious than a bad cold, the last thing you think about is sex; you want to lie in bed and drink your tea and chicken soup. You have to be healthy to be interested in sex. Also many medications can affect sexual function, such as sleeping pills, painkillers, tranquilizers, and alcohol, which is one of the most potent agents to decrease sexual function.

SEXUALITY QUIZ

We feel that it is helpful for *Pre-REtirement Planners* to take the PREP sexuality quiz as a refresher course in the reality of their bodies and their needs. As people grow older, they have a tendency to form certain rigid ideas concerning sex, and often these ideas are erroneous. Many *Pre-REtirement Planners* have registered shock after taking this quiz. They were confident they knew all the answers and could not believe they had scored so poorly. Read the questions on the quiz sheet carefully and take as long as needed to answer them. A score of 13–15 correct answers is excellent. A score of 10–12 is average and can stand improvement. A score of less than 10 suggests that you have a lot to learn, even in your retirement years.

Multiple Choice

1. Which is the most vulnerable male sexual function with increasing age?

    (a)   ability to father a child
    (b)   ejaculation
    (c)   erection
    (d)   libido
    (e)   sensation

2. Female sexual behavior in the elderly is limited by which of these?

    (a)   lack of privacy
    (b)   lack of male partners
    (c)   fear of social ostracism from peers
    (d)   disapproval by relatives
    (e)   all of these

3. Regular sexual activity in elderly people cannot help accomplish which one of the following goals?

    (a)   maintain sex hormone levels
    (b)   extend sexual functions throughout life
    (c)   be salutary in people with mild and moderate heart and lung disease
    (d)   help one lose weight
    (e)   prevent drying out of the vagina

4. Impotence in people over 65 is *least* related to which one of the following?

   (a) decrease in hormones
   (b) performance fear
   (c) taking medication
   (d) heart disease
   (e) loss of spouse

5. Which of the following illnesses may be manifested by sexual dysfunction?

   (a) diabetes
   (b) depression
   (c) anemia
   (d) obesity
   (e) all of these

True or False

_____ 6. Prostatectomy performed through the penis (transurethral) usually leads to impotence in the male.

_____ 7. Masturbation is rarely a sexual outlet for elderly people.

_____ 8. There is a higher death rate among men engaging in what some consider ''illicit sex.''

_____ 9. Orgasm is an important goal for the enjoyment of sex in the elderly.

_____ 10. The greatest cause of sexual incapacity in people over the age of 60 is poor communication with the partner.

_____ 11. Vitamin E is a useful adjunct in maintaining sexual function.

_____ 12. The best sexual position to use as you age is the ''missionary position.''

_____ 13. As men age they tend to place more emphasis upon secondary sexual stimuli such as clothes, perfume, and verbal communication.

_____ 14. The decrease in scalp hair in women is related to the decline in body estrogens.

_____ 15. Bleeding after sexual intercourse may be a serious sign of a malignancy.

Answers

1.   The answer is (c). Men have been known to father children in their 80s, even 90s. But the ability to obtain a firm erection becomes increasingly difficult with age.

2.   The answer is (e). Because women live so much longer than men, they are often widowed in their later years. In the elderly population there is a severe shortage of male partners. Also because women are more social than men they tend to live with or near friends or relatives and, in matters of sex, often suffer from lack of privacy, fear of social ostracism from peers, and the disapproval of relatives.

3.   The answer is (d). Average sexual relations burn up only about 150 calories. However, sex on a regular basis is important to the maintenance of physical and mental health.

4.   The answer is (a). The ancient remedy of taking hormone shots to improve sexual performance is usually useless. As stated earlier, men maintain a high testosterone level throughout life. Performance fear, medication, heart disease, and the loss of a spouse are the principal causes of impotence.

5.   The answer is (e). Any severe illness can result in impotence in either sex.

6.   False. The prostate operation for a benign enlarged gland, while relatively simple, frightens many men who are convinced that they will be left impotent. If the prostate enlargement is benign, their fears are unwarranted; the usual operation will not cause impotence. If, however, the prostate is cancerous and an extensive operation has to be done, the patient is usually rendered impotent.

7.   False. Masturbation is common at all ages. In the 1960s, many patients in nursing homes were forced to wear what looked like boxing gloves. Nurses had found patients masturbating and the gloves were used to stop the practice. This medieval cruelty is now illegal in all states; a room now has to be set aside where people can go by themselves or as couples. This room is known by all kinds of euphemisms: the dating room, the socializing room, and the library, among others.

8. True. Curiously, many more men die from heart attacks or strokes while engaging in sex with a woman other than their spouse.

9. False. Orgasm becomes less important as one grows older.

10. True. Poor communication between partners creates sexual difficulties at any age.

11. False. It is true in rats, but not in human beings.

12. False. The missionary position, with the man on the top, may create physical problems for the elderly. The lower back is the weakest part of our body, and most of us as we grow older develop problems in our lower back and hips. Sometimes when a woman takes too much weight on her body or the man moves in an awkward position, discomfort results. In sex, the best rule to follow is that if it feels good, do it, and if it hurts, don't do it.

13. True. Testosterone is the hormone of violence, of aggression and anger. The young man, hit with a burst of testosterone, is not always gentle or controllable. Most violent crimes are committed by young men. But as a man grows older and the hormone level goes down, he becomes less angry; he notices what clothes the woman is wearing; he becomes more appreciative of women as women. However, the opposite is happening with women. As they age they have fewer female hormones but are still making testosterone. As a result, they take on more and more aspects of the male personality.

14. True. Because the female hormones are decreasing while the male hormones remain constant, some women actually go bald, accumulate more body hair, and develop a deeper voice. This process can sometimes be reversed by taking female hormones.

15. True. Any unusual discharge, in young or old, should be immediately investigated.

NUTRITION

How many of us know what a healthy diet is? We were taught in grammar school that our bodies need a combination of protein, carbohydrate, and fat, but beyond that most of us were told little. Even most doctors are poorly educated in the science of nutrition. The *Pre-REtirement Planner*, however, stands a good chance of living a longer and healther life in retirement by learning and practicing good nutritional habits.

Are American eating habits healthy? The answer is: not very. The Japanese diet, which is rich in fish, rice, and lots of vegetables, is perhaps the world's healthiest, followed closely by the Italian diet. In Italy, spaghetti with meatballs—an American invention—does not exist. Italian chefs will throw up their arms and say, ''Why ruin perfectly good spaghetti with big hunks of hamburger?'' Most Italian sauces are very light, and pasta, an Italian staple, happens to be one of the best food sources there is. The Israeli, Greek, Spanish, and Scandinavian diets, emphasizing olive oil, bread, fish, and potatoes, are also superior to ours. It is certainly no coincidence that life expectancy in those countries significantly surpasses ours.

If you want to know how we eat in America, visit the Howard Johnson's in Terre Haute, Indiana. Big breakfast #1 consists of two eggs any style, two hotcakes, hash brown patties soaked in butter, and two crisp bacon strips. Big breakfast #2 will give you two eggs, two crisp bacon strips, two patties of hash brown potatoes with cheese sauce, an English muffin with butter, and coffee with cream. Although there is no one food on the breakfast specials that you can label as junk, putting all the ingredients together in one breakfast will give you enough fat and cholesterol to last a week.

Fat intake—and for good reason—has become a subject of concern to Americans, and until fairly recently there has been a general misunderstanding about our overconsumption of saturated fat. Saturated fat is found in red meat, butter, and cream. Suddenly we were told that too much saturated fat raises cholesterol levels, and as a result people began buying polyunsaturated fat, which is found in corn oil, vegetable oil, and margarine. Rat studies, however, have shown that poly-unsaturated fat consumed in great quantities causes cancer. It is now recommended that of the fat you consume no more than a third should be polyunsaturated. The healthiest form of fat in the human diet is mono-unsaturated, and the best sources are olive oil and peanut oil.

What should be the basis of our diet—the ideal balance of proteins, carbohydrates, and fats? Only 20 percent of our calories should be protein and less than 30% should be fat; the remaining should be in the form of complex carbohydrates—foods such as grains, rice, potatoes, wheat products, fruits, and vegetables. A diet heavy in the complex carbohydrates will supply us with all of the vitamins and minerals we need (and save us from spending a fortune for them in bottles).

Below is a list of nutrition tips we should follow, particularly as we approach retirement age:

• Try to limit intake of cholesterol to 300 milligrams a day—the amount in one egg yolk!—if your cholesterol level is above 200.

• Restrict the amount of sugar in the diet. It provides us with useless and empty calories. Cakes, sodas, candies, and jellies are some of the prime villains.

• Salt is less of a villain than sugar, unless you have high blood pressure or heart disease. Before sprinkling it liberally on your food, however, you should check with your doctor.

• Women should be sure to ingest 1,000 to 1,500 milligrams of calcium per day (green vegetables, dairy products, and fish are rich in it) because it helps to prevent osteoporosis.

• Eat less in retirement. The older we get, the fewer calories we need to maintain our proper weight. So don't waste those calories by consuming empty ones, such as sugar.

NUTRITION QUIZ

See how you fare on the nutrition quiz. A score of 13–15 correct answers is superior. A score of 10–12 is average and could stand improvement. A score of 10 or fewer suggests that you should make an appointment with your doctor to have your cholesterol checked.

Multiple Choice

1. Which one of the following portions of foods has the most calories?

>   (a)   2 slices of white bread
>   (b)   2 potatoes (baked)
>   (c)   ½ cup rice
>   (d)   ½ cup unsalted peanuts
>   (e)   1 cup of popcorn

2. Which one of the following foods is the best source of iron?

>   (a)   bran
>   (b)   whole wheat bread
>   (c)   steak
>   (d)   spinach
>   (e)   raisins

3. Which one of the following vitamins may be dangerous to take in excess of daily requirements?

>   (a)   vitamin D
>   (b)   folic acid
>   (c)   iron
>   (d)   vitamin A
>   (e)   all of these

4. Which of the following vitamins is safest when taken in excess of daily requirements?

>   (a)   vitamin B_{12}
>   (b)   vitamin E
>   (c)   vitamin C
>   (d)   vitamin K
>   (e)   none of these

True or False

____   5.   Women at age 65 need twice as much iron as men.

____   6.   On a weight-to-weight basis, fats supply more calories than carbohydrates or proteins.

_____ 7. Alcohol should not be consumed after age 72.

_____ 8. Bran and other whole grains may be useful in preventing certain types of cancer.

_____ 9. Loss of appetite is an invariable consequence of aging.

_____ 10. Pizza is a poor source of nutrition and gives one "empty calories."

_____ 11. Eggs are one food that should not be eaten as you age as they supply excessive amounts of cholesterol.

_____ 12. The older you get the easier it is to put on weight.

_____ 13. Exercise is a poor way to reduce weight.

_____ 14. The most real weight you can lose on a diet is approximately ½ pound a day.

Answers

1. The answer is (d). Two slices of bread have only about 110 calories; two baked potatoes without butter or cream about 130. One half cup of rice has about 90 calories, and one cup of popcorn only 60 calories, which makes it a favorite snack food of Weight Watchers. Eating peanuts is like eating steak. One cup has about 450 calories! It's excellent food—the fat is the right fat—but unfortunately peanuts are fattening.

2. The answer is (c). Bran and whole wheat actually inhibit iron from entering the body. Spinach—Popeye notwithstanding—has some iron, but since we can't use most of it, it's worthless. Blood banks give you raisins after you give blood because they're not about to cook you a steak.

3. The answer is (e). There are two types of vitamins, fat-soluble and water-soluble. The fat-soluble vitamins are D, A, K, and E. If you take in too much of the fat-soluble vitamins they will store up in your body and can harm you. For example, too little vitamin D will give you softening of the bone—rickets or osteomalacia—but too much of it will rob your bone of calcium. Too little vitamin A will make you go blind; too much will also make you go blind. Too little vitamin K will make you bleed, but so will too much vitamin K.

The water-soluble vitamins B and C are a little safer, but nonetheless there can be serious risks, particularly with a vitamin B_{12} deficiency, which can lead to anemia, senility, dementia, and nerve damage. If you are deficient in vitamin B_{12} and you take folic acid, the anemia improves but the nerve damage and senility grow worse. Too little vitamin B_6 will give you numbness and tingling in your hands and legs, but so will too much vitamin B_6. So the B vitamins are not quite so safe as once thought.

Iron deserves a special discussion. Most of us are under the impression that we don't get enough of it, whereas in fact many of us are in danger of iron overload. Pursuant to a law Congress passed in 1970, all of our wheat products are supplemented with iron, and the illness hemochromatosis is beginning to crop up in the United States—an oversupply of iron in the system. Hemochromatosis can result in cirrhosis of the liver, diabetes, and heart disease. All available statistics show that this illness is on the rise, because with aging we keep accumulating iron, and unless we bleed we have no way of getting rid of our body's share of iron.

Except for women who need iron to replace what is lost through menstruating, no one needs it as a supplement. If you're iron-deficient it's because you have been bleeding, but normal people as they grow older keep accumulating more and more iron.

4.   The answer is (a), and this will come as a shock to all of the C users in this country. When you're feeling run-down and go to a doctor wanting a shot of something to pep you up, he is likely to give you a shot of B_{12}. It is the safest of all the vitamins. Although C is relatively safe, in some people it can cause kidney stones or diarrhea.

5.   False. Women who have stopped menstruating need no more iron than do men.

6.   True. Each gram of fat is worth nine calories. Each gram of carbohydrates or proteins is worth only four calories.

7.   False. As a matter of fact, those who live the longest have one or two alcoholic drinks per day, each drink containing either 1¼ ounces of 80 proof liquor, or 4 to 6 ounces of wine, or 12 ounces of beer (16 ounces of light beer). A moderate intake of alcohol seems to lower cholesterol and to raise the HDL, or the good cholesterol.

8.   True. Particularly cancer of the colon.

9. False. Lack of appetite is a sign that something is physically or emotionally wrong. We should be hungry all of our lives.

10. False. Pizza happens to be *almost a perfect food.* It is a complex carbohydrate, with cheese, tomato, and olive oil.

11. False. If your cholesterol is low—around 150—you can eat all the eggs you want.

12. True (alas!).

13. True. As we grow older we should exercise no more than 2,500–3,000 calories per week. It takes 3,500 calories to lose one pound; thus we cannot depend on exercise to lose weight. We must eat less.

14. True. Remember, it takes 3,500 calories to lose a pound, so if you cut out your caloric intake completely you can lose perhaps half a pound. People on quick weight-loss diets think they're losing weight but they're not. They are actually putting out a lot of water so that at the end of two weeks they can say, "Look, I lost twenty pounds!" It's a dangerous practice.

A THIRD OF YOUR LIFE

For a person to live well into extreme old age it is important to have a reasonably good diet, reasonable amounts of exercise, and sound health habits. We must try to stay happy by staying sociable and developing loving and close relationships with other people *throughout life*. From all current demographics it is clear that most Americans in retirement can now expect to live into their 80s, which means that the *Pre-REtirement Planner* will have from 20 to 30 years ahead of him or her. In planning for retirement it is important to remember that you still have a third of your life to live. A third of a life span is a long time, and you have to ask yourself not only what you expect to do with those years but how you can stay healthy and vigorous during your senior adulthood.

The chances are you will be healthy. There is every reason to hope that you will be happy and at least modestly well off.

By following simple guidelines, common sense, and restraint, your retirement can be a success!

Appendix

PRE-RETIREMENT
PLANNING WORKSHEETS

Before you begin to prepare your pre-retirement financial plans, gather together the following information:

1.   Last year's federal and state income tax returns.

2.   Your record of estimated tax returns for the current year, if applicable.

3.   Any files of supporting information, receipts, and bills for these income tax returns.

4.   Your current checking and savings account records listing the payee, amount of each check drawn, deposits and withdrawals, and transfers to and from other accounts for the last year.

5.   Copies of your latest statements from checking accounts, savings accounts, money market accounts, mutual funds, and stock-brokers.

6.   Any inventory of stock certificates, bonds, real estate, and other investments that are not included in periodic statements. (You should know the date purchased, purchase price, and current dividends, interest, or other income for each investment.)

7. An inventory of personal items and collectibles which you would consider it appropriate to sell to help finance your retirement. This may include antique furniture, art, jewelry, furs, and any type of collectibles.

Your personal records should be in good order as you approach retirement. This appendix will provide you with a place to record all of the vital information you need. Keep this information current by reviewing it each year!

Please duplicate these planning worksheets for your convenience.

A P P E N D I X

PERSONAL RECORDS _____

NAME _____
        first   middle   last

DATE OF BIRTH _____
        day   month   year

WHERE BORN _____
        city   state

SOCIAL SECURITY NUMBER _____

BIRTH CERTIFICATE:
Original, filed where _____

Copy, filed where _____

RELIGION _____

DATE & PLACE OF MARRIAGE _____

LOCATION OF MARRIAGE CERTIFICATE _____

IF PREVIOUSLY MARRIED,
LOCATION OF DIVORCE OR SEPARATION PAPERS _____

NAMES OF PARENTS _____
        mother's maiden name   father

PARENTS' PLACE OF BIRTH _____
        mother   father

POWER OF ATTORNEY:
I have (have not) executed a power of attorney, date

_____
(month, day, year)

naming _____
(agent or attorney in fact)

_____
(address)

A P P E N D I X

Income Tax:

Copies of my federal and state income tax returns and related papers are located at:

_____

Other tax information:
Copies of _____ tax returns and related papers are
                    (property, etc.)

located at _____

_____

Location of passbooks for savings accounts: _____

_____

_____

Location of statements and canceled checks for checking accounts: _____

_____

_____

SPOUSE'S PERSONAL RECORDS

NAME
_____
        first   middle   last

DATE OF BIRTH
_____
        day   month   year

WHERE BORN
_____
        city   state

SOCIAL SECURITY NUMBER
_____

BIRTH CERTIFICATE:
Original, filed where
_____

Copy, filed where
_____

RELIGION
_____

DATE & PLACE OF MARRIAGE
_____

LOCATION OF MARRIAGE CERTIFICATE
_____

IF PREVIOUSLY MARRIED,
LOCATION OF DIVORCE OR SEPARATION PAPERS
_____

NAMES OF PARENTS
_____
        mother's maiden name   father

PARENTS' PLACE OF BIRTH
_____
                mother   father

POWER OF ATTORNEY:
I have (have not) executed a power of attorney, date

_____
                (month, day, year)

naming
_____
                (agent or attorney in fact)

_____
                (address)

A P P E N D I X

Spouse's Income Tax:

Copies of my federal and state income tax returns and related papers are located at:

_____

Other tax information:

Copies of _____ tax returns and related papers are
                        (property, etc.)

located at _____

_____

Location of passbooks for savings accounts: _____

_____

_____

Location of statements and canceled checks for checking accounts: _____

_____

_____

A P P E N D I X

PERSONAL RECORDS

CHILDREN AND GRANDCHILDREN

NAMES	DATES OF BIRTH	ADDRESSES & TELEPHONE NUMBERS

A P P E N D I X

	ITEM	WHERE KEPT	$ ESTIMATE	INSURED
JEWELRY	1.			
	2.			
	3.			
	4.			
	5.			
	6.			
COLLECTIBLES	1.			
	2.			
	3.			
	4.			
	5.			
	6.			
OTHER	1.			
	2.			
	3.			
	4.			
	5.			
	6.			

A P P E N D I X

MISCELLANEOUS RECORDS

IN NAME OF   NUMBER & EXPIRATION DATE

SOCIAL SECURITY CARD(s) _____

_____

DRIVER'S LICENSE(s) _____

_____

_____

_____

CREDIT CARDS _____

_____

_____

_____

CHARGE ACCOUNTS _____

_____

_____

_____

A P P E N D I X

EMPLOYMENT RECORD

COMPANY & ADDRESS	JOB TITLE	DATES	
(Start with most recent)		To	From

1. _____

2. _____

3. _____

4. _____

5. _____

6. _____

7. _____

8. _____

9. _____

10. _____

11. _____

APPENDIX

SPOUSE'S EMPLOYMENT RECORD

COMPANY & ADDRESS (Start with most recent)	JOB TITLE	DATES To	From

1. _____

2. _____

3. _____

4. _____

5. _____

6. _____

7. _____

8. _____

9. _____

10. _____

11. _____

A P P E N D I X

<u>MILITARY RECORD</u>

<u>BRANCH OF SERVICE</u> _____

<u>SERIAL NUMBER</u> _____

<u>DATES OF SERVICE</u> _____
from   to

<u>SEPARATED WITH RANK OF</u> _____

<u>LOCATION OF DISCHARGE PAPERS</u> _____

<u>OTHER DETAILS, CITATIONS, ETC.</u> _____

_____

<u>SPOUSE'S MILITARY RECORD</u>

<u>BRANCH OF SERVICE</u> _____

<u>SERIAL NUMBER</u> _____

<u>DATES OF SERVICE</u> _____
from   to

<u>SEPARATED WITH RANK OF</u> _____

<u>LOCATION OF DISCHARGE PAPERS</u> _____

<u>OTHER DETAILS, CITATIONS, ETC.</u> _____

_____

A P P E N D I X

PROFESSIONAL ADVISERS

NAME   ADDRESS & TELEPHONE

PHYSICIAN _____

DENTIST _____

BROKER/INVESTMENT ADVISER _____

_____

ACCOUNTANT _____

ATTORNEY _____

CLERGYMAN _____

WILL

LOCATION OF LATEST WILL _____

DATE_____

EXECUTOR _____ ADDRESS _____

ATTORNEY _____ ADDRESS _____

A P P E N D I X

SPOUSE'S PROFESSIONAL ADVISERS

NAME   ADDRESS & TELEPHONE

PHYSICIAN _____

DENTIST _____

BROKER/INVESTMENT ADVISER _____

_____

ACCOUNTANT _____

ATTORNEY _____

CLERGYMAN _____

WILL

LOCATION OF LATEST WILL _____

DATE_____

EXECUTOR _____ ADDRESS _____

ATTORNEY _____ ADDRESS _____

A P P E N D I X

BANK ACCOUNTS

NAME & ADDRESS,
BANK/CREDIT UNION/
SAVINGS & LOAN, ETC.   ACCOUNTS #   OTHER NAMES ON ACCOUNT

1. _____

2. _____

3. _____

4. _____

Please note: It is policy on the part of most, if not all, banks to freeze joint accounts on notification of death of one of the owners.

SAFETY DEPOSIT BOX

NAME & ADDRESS OF BANK _____

BOX NO. _____ LOCATION OF KEYS _____ (Do not indicate this in writing. Tell someone orally.)

_____

NAMES & ADDRESSES
OF PERSONS WITH KEYS _____

_____

_____

Cautionary note: Safety deposit boxes are also sealed on notification of death. So wills, insurance policies, and other documents that may be needed at that time should not be kept in such boxes.

A P P E N D I X

<u>INVESTMENTS</u>

STOCKS, BONDS, OTHER SECURITIES

TYPE OF SECURITY	COMPANY	DATE BOUGHT	NUMBER OF SHARES	COST PER SHARE	IN NAME OF

A P P E N D I X

INVESTMENTS

REAL ESTATE

KIND OF PROPERTY _____

WHERE LOCATED _____

TITLE _____

IN WHOSE NAME _____

DATE ACQUIRED _____

COST _____

TENANT(S) NAME & ADDRESS _____

_____

MORTGAGE AMOUNT _____

MORTGAGE TERM _____

MONTHLY PAYMENT _____

DATE PAYMENT DUE _____

A P P E N D I X

OTHER INVESTMENTS

KIND OF INVESTMENT _____

AMOUNT INVESTED _____

TERMS OF PAYMENT: INTEREST; WHEN DUE _____

FROM WHOM: NAME & ADDRESS _____

_____

ANNUITIES

Annuities are payable as follows:

DESCRIPTION _____

PAYABLE TO _____

ADDRESS _____

CURRENT AMOUNT $ _____ per month

DESCRIPTION: _____

PAYABLE TO _____

ADDRESS _____

AMOUNT PAYABLE $_____ per month (fixed amount)

A P P E N D I X

OBLIGATIONS

1. OUTSTANDING PERSONAL LOAN(S)

AMOUNT OF LOAN _____

OWED TO WHOM (NAME & ADDRESS) _____

_____

TERMS OF PAYMENT, INTEREST _____

WHEN DUE IN FULL _____

2. OUTSTANDING BANK LOAN(S)

AMOUNT OF LOAN _____

NAME & ADDRESS OF BANK _____

TERMS OF PAYMENT, INTEREST _____

WHEN DUE IN FULL _____

3. OTHER MEDIUM- TO LONG-TERM OBLIGATIONS

AMOUNT OF OBLIGATION _____

DESCRIPTION; TO WHOM OWED _____

_____

Note: List life insurance loans on ''Life Insurance Policies'' page.

A P P E N D I X

MEDICAL HISTORY

RECORD OF PREVIOUS ILLNESS/OPERATIONS, ETC.:

Nature of Illness   Physician   Dates   Remarks

REGULAR MEDICATIONS TAKEN

BLOOD TYPE

ALLERGIES TO MEDICATIONS

LOCATION OF X-RAYS, OTHER MEDICAL RECORDS

A P P E N D I X

SPOUSE'S MEDICAL HISTORY

RECORD OF PREVIOUS ILLNESS/OPERATIONS, ETC.:

Nature of Illness   Physician   Dates   Remarks

_____

_____

_____

_____

_____

_____

REGULAR MEDICATIONS TAKEN _____

_____

BLOOD TYPE _____

ALLERGIES TO MEDICATIONS _____

_____

LOCATION OF X-RAYS, OTHER MEDICAL RECORDS _____

_____

A P P E N D I X

<u>MEDICAL/HOSPITAL INSURANCE</u>

(Other Than Medicare/Medicaid)

1. INSURING COMPANY _____

KIND OF POLICY (hospital benefits, nursing care, etc.) _____

_____

_____

POLICY # _____

BENEFICIARIES _____

_____

PREMIUM & DATE DUE _____

2. INSURING COMPANY _____

KIND OF POLICY (hospital benefits, nursing care, etc.) _____

_____

_____

POLICY # _____

BENEFICIARIES _____

_____

PREMIUM & DATE DUE _____

A P P E N D I X

MEDICAL/HOSPITAL INSURANCE

(Other Than Medicare/Medicaid)

3. INSURING COMPANY _____

KIND OF POLICY (hospital benefits, nursing care, etc.) _____

_____

_____

POLICY # _____

BENEFICIARIES _____

_____

PREMIUM & DATE DUE _____

A P P E N D I X

LIFE INSURANCE POLICIES

	YOURSELF	SPOUSE
NAME OF COMPANY		
POLICY #		
FACE AMOUNT		
CASH VALUE		
OUTSTANDING LOAN AMOUNT		
BENEFICIARIES		
PREMIUM & DUE DATE		
INSURANCE AGENT		
POLICY TYPE (term, whole, etc.).		

NAME OF COMPANY		
POLICY #		
FACE AMOUNT		
CASH VALUE		
OUTSTANDING LOAN AMOUNT		
BENEFICIARIES		
PREMIUM & DUE DATE		
INSURANCE AGENT		
POLICY TYPE (term, whole, etc.)		

LIFE INSURANCE POLICIES

                        YOURSELF   SPOUSE
_____

NAME OF COMPANY _____

POLICY # _____

FACE AMOUNT _____

CASH VALUE _____

OUTSTANDING LOAN AMOUNT _____

BENEFICIARIES _____

_____

PREMIUM & DUE DATE _____

INSURANCE AGENT _____

POLICY TYPE (term, whole, etc.). _____

_____

NAME OF COMPANY _____

POLICY # _____

FACE AMOUNT _____

CASH VALUE _____

OUTSTANDING LOAN AMOUNT _____

BENEFICIARIES _____

_____

PREMIUM & DUE DATE _____

INSURANCE AGENT _____

POLICY TYPE (term, whole, etc.) _____

A P P E N D I X

LIFE INSURANCE REVIEW

1.   Before retirement, contact your Benefits Department to make sure that the beneficiaries shown on your policies are completely up to date.

2.   In the case of other insurance policies:

    a.   Be sure that each policy shows the correct beneficiaries.

    b.   The age of the insured person must be correctly given, and also must be provable.

    c.   Look into taking out a loan on the cash surrender value.

3.   Investigate the possibility of having your insurer pay a higher rate of interest or annuity than that shown on the policy—something to explore with older policies.

4.   Contact your insurance agent (if you haven't done so recently) to get a complete listing of the options available to your beneficiaries: lump sum; funds left in at interest, and what rate; conversion into an annuity, etc.

APPENDIX

HOMEOWNERS/PROPERTY/LIABILITY INSURANCE

1. INSURING COMPANY _____

POLICY NUMBER _____

POLICY AMOUNT & DEDUCTIBLES _____

PREMIUM & DATE DUE _____

WHAT THE POLICY COVERS _____

2. INSURING COMPANY _____

POLICY NUMBER _____

POLICY AMOUNT & DEDUCTIBLES _____

PREMIUM & DATE DUE _____

WHAT THE POLICY COVERS _____

A P P E N D I X

AUTOMOTIVE & CASUALTY INSURANCE

1. INSURING COMPANY _____

POLICY NUMBER _____

NAMES OF INSURED _____

POLICY AMOUNT _____

PREMIUM & DATE DUE _____

WHAT THE POLICY COVERS _____

2. INSURING COMPANY _____

POLICY NUMBER _____

NAMES OF INSURED _____

POLICY AMOUNT _____

PREMIUM & DATE DUE _____

WHAT THE POLICY COVERS _____

A P P E N D I X

FUNERAL ARRANGEMENTS

NAME _____
         first   middle   last

RELIGION _____

I HAVE SELECTED INTERMENT _____ CREMATION _____

I HAVE GIVEN DIRECTIONS FOR ARRANGEMENTS TO _____

_____
                  name and address

BURIAL PLOT LOCATED _____

INDIVIDUALS TO BE INFORMED _____

_____

_____

_____

ORGANIZATIONS TO BE INFORMED (business, fraternal, club, etc.) ____

_____

_____

INSTRUCTIONS REGARDING SERVICES _____

_____

_____

House of worship and clergy—Consult before making funeral arrangements.

_____
clergy   telephone—house of worship

_____
address   telephone—home

VETERANS ADMINISTRATION

A spouse may be eligible for a veteran's death pension and burial allowances will be payable. As a general rule, the funeral director will assist in claiming this benefit.

Location of my personal VA papers: _____

Nearest VA Office:

_____
(name and address)   telephone

A P P E N D I X

SPOUSE'S FUNERAL ARRANGEMENTS

NAME
_____
      first   middle   last

RELIGION _____

I HAVE SELECTED INTERMENT _____ CREMATION _____

I HAVE GIVEN DIRECTIONS FOR ARRANGEMENTS TO _____

_____
                    name and address

BURIAL PLOT LOCATED _____

INDIVIDUALS TO BE INFORMED _____

_____

_____

_____

ORGANIZATIONS TO BE INFORMED (business, fraternal, club, etc.)

_____

_____

INSTRUCTIONS REGARDING SERVICES _____

_____

_____

House of worship and clergy—Consult before making funeral arrangements.

_____
clergy   telephone—house of worship

_____
address   telephone—home

VETERANS ADMINISTRATION

A spouse may be eligible for a veteran's death pension and burial allowances will be payable. As a general rule, the funeral director will assist in claiming this benefit.

Location of my personal VA papers: _____

Nearest VA Office:

_____
(name and address)   telephone

FINANCIAL PROFILE WORKSHEETS

These sheets can be removed from the book, duplicated if necessary, and used to work out the basic financial data required for planning.

RETIREMENT NET WORTH PROFILE

ASSETS	Today	At Retirement
1. Cash on hand and in bank accounts, certificates of deposit, etc., which you can gain access to immediately, even if there is a penalty		
2. Securities, including bonds, common and preferred stocks, government securities, mutual funds, etc.		
3. Cash value of company employee investment fund or other company savings plans, etc.		
4. Cash value of IRA accounts and Keoghs (HR 19) Husband: Wife:		
5. Cash surrender values of life insurance policies		
6. Value of your home		
7. Value of any other real estate investments, summer houses, etc.		
8. Value of your full- or part-time business		
9. Value of your cars		
10. Value of any collectibles, gold, jewelry, furs, etc.		
TOTAL ASSETS		

LIABILITIES	Today	At Retirement
1. Remaining principal due on mortgages on your home and any real estate investments		
2. Balance of car loan		
3. Balance of any bank loans, personal debt, credit cards, charge accounts, etc.		
TOTAL LIABILITIES		
RETIREMENT NET WORTH		

CASH EXPENSE PROFILE

	Today	At Retirement
A. Housing expenses		
1. Mortgage		
2. Real estate taxes—principal home		
3. Real estate taxes—summer home		
4. Utilities		
5. Maintenance and repairs		
6. Insurance		
TOTAL HOUSING EXPENSES		
B. Food and personal expenses		
1. Dining at home		
2. Dining out		
3. Personal care		
4. Clothing		
5. Recreation		
6. Furniture, appliances, etc.		
7. All other		
TOTAL FOOD AND PERSONAL EXPENSES		

	Today	At Retirement
C. Automobile expenses		
1. Loan payments, or savings to replace auto		
2. Fuel, maintenance, and repairs		
3. Insurance		
TOTAL AUTOMOBILE EXPENSES		
D. Travel expenses		
E. Life insurance—paid-up at age 65		
F. Medical, dental, and accident insurance		
G. Gifts and contributions		
H. Savings		
TOTAL CASH EXPENSES		

CASH INCOME PROFILE

	Today	At Retirement
A. From today to retirement		
1. Net income from salaries and wages after all tax and other deductions		
2. Interest received from savings accounts, certificates of deposit, etc.		
3. Dividends received from investments in securities		
4. Other income		
5. Less estimated federal, state, and local taxes on items 2–4 above		
TOTAL CASH INCOME FROM TODAY TO RETIREMENT		

	Today	At Retirement
B. Cash income after retirement		
1. Retirement income		
a. Social Security (partly taxable)		
b. Company pension plan (all taxable)		
2. Interest and dividends from A2 and A3		
3. Other income from A4, if applicable		
4. Less federal, state, and local taxes on all of the above		
CASH INCOME BEFORE USE OF OTHER ASSETS		
LESS: CASH EXPENSES AT RETIREMENT FROM CASH EXPENSE PROFILE		
ADDITIONAL AFTER-TAX INCOME REQUIRED TO MEET CASH EXPENSES AT RETIREMENT		

continues next page

	Today	At Retirement
C. Sources of additional after-tax income		
1. Withdrawals from savings accounts, proceeds from certificates of deposit, and sale of securities (partly taxable)		
2. Withdrawals from IRAs, company employee fund, or other savings plans (partly taxable)		
3. Less federal, state, and local taxes on above		
TOTAL ADDITIONAL AFTER-TAX INCOME REQUIRED		

Index